Best Hikes St. Louis

The Greatest Views, Wildlife, and Forest Strolls

SECOND EDITION

JD TANNER AND EMILY RESSLER-TANNER

FALCONGUIDES

GUILFORD, CONNECTICUT

An imprint of The Rowman & Littlefield Publishing Group, Inc.
4501 Forbes Blvd., Ste. 200
Lanham, MD 20706
www.rowman.com

Falcon and FalconGuides are registered trademarks and Make Adventure Your Story is a trademark of The Rowman & Littlefield Publishing Group, Inc.

Distributed by NATIONAL BOOK NETWORK

Copyright © 2018 The Rowman & Littlefield Publishing Group, Inc.
A previous edition of this book was published by Falcon Publishing, Inc. in 2012.

Maps © The Rowman & Littlefield Publishing Group. Inc.
All photos by JD Tanner and Emily Ressler-Tanner unless otherwise noted.

British Library Cataloguing-in-Publication Information Available

Library of Congress Cataloguing-in-Publication Information available

ISBN 978-1-4930-2974-7 (paperback)
ISBN 978-1-4930-2975-4 (e-book)

♾™ The paper used in this publication meets the minimum requirements of American National Standard for Information Sciences—Permanence of Paper for Printed Library Materials, ANSI / NISO Z39.48-1992.

Printed in the United States of America

Contents

Overview Map

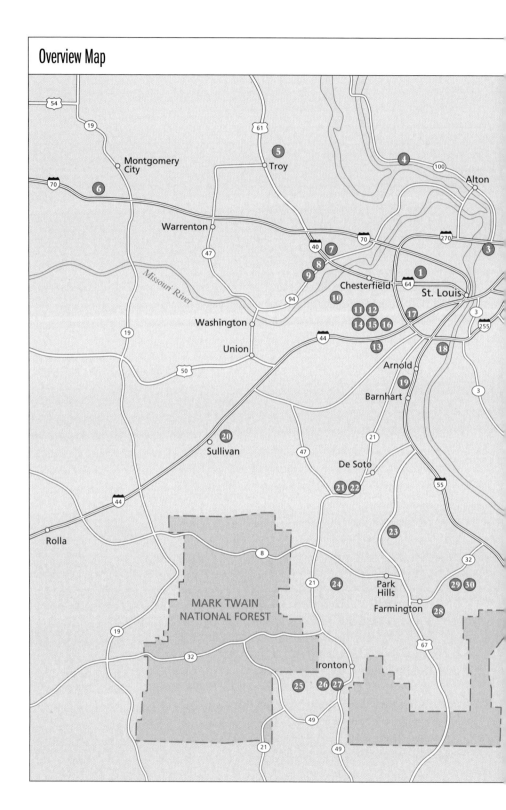

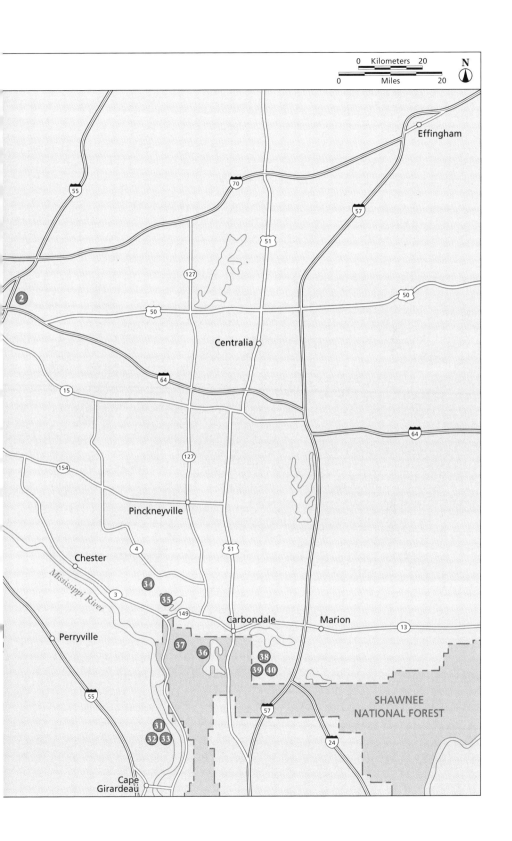

Acorn

Acknowledgments

We would like to thank all of our friends and family in the St. Louis and southern Illinois areas who offered us a place to rest, a bed to sleep in, and/or a meal to eat with them. Special thanks to all the Missouri State Park, St. Louis County Park, Missouri Department of Conservation, Illinois State Park, and Shawnee National Forest land managers who patiently answered our questions, pointed us toward the very best trails, and carefully reviewed the trail descriptions for this guide. We would also like to thank Donna Batson, Janet Wade, Ashley Sneathen, and, of course, our two best trail companions, Arnie and Aspen, for accompanying us on many of the trails in and around St. Louis. Your company, humor, and enthusiasm were very much appreciated.

Finally, we would like to thank all of our friends at FalconGuides, particularly Max Phelps, Dave Legere, and Julie Marsh, for their support, encouragement, and for making a book out of our rough manuscript.

We hope that you enjoy hiking the trails in this guide as much as we do!

Introduction

Welcome to the Show Me State. As the unofficial state slogan indicates, Missourians need to see in order to believe. We believe that one look at the pictures in this guide will convince you that Missouri is indeed a hiking destination to be reckoned with. For more than a century, St. Louis was considered the gateway to the wild and wondrous West. Today it is a modern city, offering a wide range of recreational opportunities.

This guidebook will show you the best trails the St. Louis area has to offer. Whether you live here or you're just visiting, you will be surprised by the variety of trails in this unique area.

When one reads about "the best" towns for outdoor recreation in the United States, St. Louis rarely finds itself on the list. Luckily, St. Louis–area residents, and now you, know better. The rolling hills of the Ozarks, the towering bluffs along the many rivers, the woodland bottoms and floodplains, and the glacier-carved formations in southern Illinois create a diverse backdrop for the hikes found in this guidebook. With this guide, you will discover that St. Louis is in fact a city full of hiking opportunities.

This guide lists easy, moderate, and more challenging hikes within 100 miles of the St. Louis metropolitan area that can meet the needs of new and veteran hikers alike. Some of the hikes can be found within the city of St. Louis, others are found south and west of the city on the edges of the Ozarks, and a few more can be found just across the Mississippi River in southern Illinois.

Founded by French traders in 1764, the city of St. Louis is currently the second-largest city in Missouri. It is located on the eastern boundary of the state, just below the confluence of the Missouri and Mississippi Rivers. This prime location made St. Louis a center for the fur-trading industry, as well as a major transportation hub, during the early part of the nineteenth century. St. Louis played an important role in the westward expansion of the United States. So many crossed through St. Louis on their journeys west that the city became known as the Gateway to the West.

MISSOURI FUN FACTS

State capital: Jefferson City

State animal: mule

State bird: bluebird

State insect: honeybee

State tree: flowering dogwood

State flower: hawthorn

State song: "Missouri Waltz"

State nickname: Show Me State

Highest elevation: Taum Sauk Mountain (1,772 feet)

◀ *Janet Wade and her trail pup, Darcy, enjoying one of the many trails in St. Louis*

Cahokia Mounds Nature/Culture Trail (hike 2)

Today, the greater St. Louis area population is pushing almost three million people. The city boasts many attractions, such as the Jefferson National Expansion Memorial, which includes the Gateway Arch and Museum of Westward Expansion and the Old Court House, site of the 1847 and 1850 trials in the pivotal Dred Scott case. St. Louis is also home to the Ulysses S. Grant National Historical Site, Missouri Botanical Gardens, and St. Louis Zoo.

The landscape in and around St. Louis is almost as fascinating as its history. The Ozarks extend south and west from St. Louis throughout southern Missouri and into northern Arkansas, eastern Oklahoma, and southeastern Kansas. The Ozarks include some of the most beautiful rolling landscapes in the United States and are also home to several Ozark National Scenic Riverways, such as the spring-fed Current River and the Jack's Fork River. In addition to these two gorgeous rivers, visitors to the area should know that Missouri is home to the country's largest natural spring, Big Spring, which flows at an average of 284 million gallons per day. The ecologically diverse, hilly, and sometimes rugged countryside of southern Illinois offers not only great hiking, but also canoeing, rock climbing, horseback riding, camping, fishing, and many more opportunities for outdoor recreation.

Featured in the pages of this book are forty of the best hikes in and around the St. Louis area. We have done our best to include a little of something for everyone. Hikes for families, for trail runners, for scenic views, and for pets have all been included and should be considered an introduction to the areas and a starting point to continue your explorations. We have also included points of interest near the hikes to give visitors a chance to fully appreciate the unique areas included in this guide.

Weather

Have you ever heard the expression "If you don't like the weather now, just wait five minutes?" Well, that expression truly applies to St. Louis.

The weather in the St. Louis area consists of a mild spring, with temperatures typically ranging from cool to warm. While occasionally muggy and typically wet, spring can be an excellent time to hike in this area. Trail conditions can be quite muddy during the early spring, especially for hikes that are in or near floodplains.

The biggest concern for spring weather in St. Louis is the chance for thunderstorms, hail, and/or tornadoes. Missouri storms can be deadly and hikers should heed any storm watches or warnings issued in and around the area. A "severe thunderstorm watch" will be issued if conditions are favorable for a severe thunderstorm. A "severe thunderstorm warning" will be issued if a storm is producing dangerously large hail or high winds capable of causing significant damage. A "tornado watch" will be issued when the conditions are right for a tornado to form. A "tornado warning" will be issued once a tornado has been sighted or picked up on radar.

According to the National Weather Service, the best place to be when severe weather strikes is a sturdy structure. Since this is often not a possibility for hikers, we

SEVERE WEATHER TIPS

If there is less than 30 seconds between the time that you see lightning and the time that you hear thunder, you should take shelter indoors. If you cannot take shelter indoors, move to a safer location, away from trees, fences, and poles. Assume the lightning position—squat low to the ground, on the balls of your feet—and stay there for 30 minutes after the last flash of lightning.

If caught outside during a tornado, look for a ditch or depression to take cover in. Lie flat and cover your head with your hands. Be aware of flying debris and falling trees. Signs of an approaching tornado include a dark and often greenish sky, large and heavy hail, and a loud roar often described as similar to that of an approaching freight train.

Storms still pose a threat in early summer, but as the summer progresses, the weather tends to be less wet, sometimes very hot, and almost always humid. Hikers who choose to go out in the mid to late summer might consider early morning hikes, as high temperatures and humidity usually set in by midmorning.

have included some of the National Weather Service's recommendations for what to do if you are outdoors when severe weather strikes.

If you are outdoors during a thunderstorm and a sturdy shelter is not available, find a low spot away from trees, fences, and poles. Avoid areas where flooding is possible. If you are in a wooded area, take shelter under the shortest trees, but avoid touching any tree trunks. Assume a "lightning position" by squatting low to the ground, on the balls of your feet. If you have a sleeping pad or backpack,

WEATHER AVERAGES FOR ST. LOUIS

Month	High	Low	Rainfall
January	38	21	2.01
February	45	26	2.06
March	55	36	3.70
April	66	47	3.82
May	77	57	3.92
June	86	66	3.73
July	91	71	3.78
August	88	69	3.70
September	81	61	2.69
October	69	49	2.81
November	54	48	4.06
December	42	27	2.56

(Statistics from the Weather Channel)

Fall scenery from Hughes Mountain (hike 24)

place it between your feet and the ground. Minimize your contact with the ground and make yourself the smallest possible target.

Fall can be downright gorgeous in St. Louis. Daytime temperatures in the low to mid-70s along with the fall foliage can amount to some amazing scenic hikes. Fall hiking cannot be encouraged enough. St. Louis has its fair share of cold and snowy days in the winter, but if you don't mind hiking when there are no leaves on the trees, winter can be a very enjoyable time to hike here as well. Those who hike in the winter will enjoy more views of the rolling Ozarks and will typically have the trails almost all to themselves.

Ideal times for hiking in St. Louis are early to late spring and mid to late fall. Mix in the handful of cooler days in the summer and some occasionally warm winter days, and a person can enjoy many ideal hiking days per year in and around St. Louis.

Hazards

There are a few hazards to be aware of and prepare for when hiking in the St. Louis area. Poison ivy, a year-round hazard, might be the most common and most annoying issue hikers will come across while hiking in and around St. Louis. Poison ivy has been found in every county in Missouri, and it is estimated that somewhere between 50 and 70 percent of people experience a physical reaction after coming in contact with the plant. Poison ivy can grow as a woody shrub up to 6 feet high or as a vine that clings to other trees and shrubs. While the old expression "Leaves of three, let it be" is good advice to follow, there are several other three-leaf plants growing in the

The bright-green, notched leaves of poison ivy

St. Louis area, so it is important to educate yourself about poison ivy before hitting the trail. Poison ivy can be found on almost every hike in this book.

Ticks are most abundant in St. Louis during the spring and summer. There are many different types of ticks, but the two most common in Missouri are the lone star tick and the American dog tick. Ticks have been known to carry, and occasionally spread, ailments such as Lyme disease, Rocky Mountain spotted fever, and tularemia. Although ticks are unavoidable, they are not a reason to avoid hiking in the spring and summer seasons. Hikers should wear light-colored clothing to help detect ticks visually, use repellant that is proven effective against ticks, periodically check for ticks, and do a complete body check on yourself and your pet after every hike. During the spring and summer, ticks can be found on every hike in this book.

There are fifty different species of mosquitoes in Missouri and Illinois, and the most common concern with mosquitoes is West Nile virus. It is estimated that only 1 percent of mosquitoes carry West Nile virus and only 1 percent of people bitten will actually contract the virus. Like ticks, mosquitoes should not be a reason to avoid hiking in the spring or summer seasons. Hikers simply need to be aware and be prepared. Things to consider when trying to avoid mosquitoes are: use an insect repellant, wear long pants and a long-sleeved shirt, avoid hiking at dawn or dusk, and don't wear perfume or cologne when hiking. Mosquitoes can be found on every hike in this book and can be quite abundant on the hikes located near floodplains.

Poisonous snakes are the fourth and final common hazard found on the hikes in this book. Most of the snakes in the St. Louis area are harmless; however, hikers should be aware that several species of venomous snakes do inhabit the area. Your chances of being bitten by a poisonous snake in the United States are very, very low. Fewer than

Ringneck snake on the River Scene Trail (hike 16)

8,000 people are bitten every year by a venomous snake, most while trying to handle or kill the snake, and fewer than five of those people die.

Missouri is home to five different species of venomous snakes: The Osage copperhead, western cottonmouth (water moccasin), timber rattlesnake, eastern Massasauga rattlesnake (swamp rattler), and western pygmy rattlesnake (ground rattler) can all be found in or near the St. Louis area. The Osage copperhead and timber rattlesnake are the two venomous snakes that a hiker is most likely to encounter. Their "arrow-shaped" heads identify them as poisonous snakes. Three of the five venomous snakes in Missouri are rattlesnakes and can be easily identified by the rattling noise they make when they feel threatened. Hikers should wear protective footwear, never place hands under rocks or logs, keep an eye on the ground while hiking, and never attempt to handle or kill snakes in order to avoid being bitten.

Other hazards you may encounter include (but are not limited to) drop-offs along bluffs, thunderstorms, tornadoes, and heat-related illnesses.

Be Prepared

"Be prepared." The Boy Scouts say it, Leave No Trace says it, and the best outdoor people say it. Being prepared won't completely keep you out of harm's way when outdoors, but it will minimize the chances of finding yourself there. That being said, here are some things to consider:

- Familiarize yourself with the basics of first aid (bites, stings, sprains, and breaks), and carry a first-aid kit and know how to use it.
- Hydrate! No matter where or when you are hiking, you should always be carrying water with you. A standard is 2 liters per person per day.
- Be prepared to treat water on longer hikes. Rivers and streams are not safe to drink directly from in the St. Louis area. Iodine tablets are small, light, and easy to carry.
- Carry a backpack to store the ten essentials: map, compass, sunglasses/sunscreen, extra food and water, extra clothes, headlamp/flashlight, first-aid kit, fire starter, matches, and knife.
- Pack your cellphone (on vibrate) as a safety backup.
- Keep an eye on the kids. Having them carry a whistle, just in case, isn't the worst idea.
- Bring a leash, doggie bags, and extra water for your pets.

Leave No Trace

This hiking guide will take you to historical sites, conservation areas, national natural landmarks, and many other places of natural and cultural significance. For that reason, the importance of Leave No Trace cannot be stressed enough. You are encouraged to carefully plan your trip so that you know as much as you possibly can about the area you will be visiting. Being aware of the weather forecast, trail conditions, and water availability are just a few important factors to planning a successful trip.

Red bud trees blooming in spring

Once you begin your hike, do your best to stick to trails so you do not inadvertently trample sensitive vegetation. Be prepared to pack out any trash that you bring with you, and remember that it never hurts to carry out trash that others may have left behind. Be extra careful when visiting sites of historical and natural importance. Leave everything as you found it, and never remove artifacts found in these sensitive areas.

Consider your impact on wildlife as you visit their homes and be sure not to feed them, as this act is unhealthy for wildlife and dangerous for people. Respect other visitors and users as well by keeping your pets on a leash, stepping to the side of the trail to allow others to pass, and keeping noise to a minimum.

For more information on enjoying the outdoors responsibly, please contact the Leave No Trace Center for Outdoor Ethics at (800) 332-4100 or visit their website at www.LNT.org.

Land Management

The following agencies manage the public lands where the hikes in this book are located and can be contacted if you have any questions and concerns before visiting.

Illinois Department of Natural Resources, Office of Land Management, 1 Natural Resources Way, Springfield, IL 62702; (217) 782-6302; www.dnr.illinois.gov

Illinois State Parks (managed by the Illinois Department of Natural Resources), Office of Land Management, 1 Natural Resources Way, Springfield, IL 62702; (217) 782-6302; www.dnr.illinois.gov

Missouri Department of Conservation, Conservation Headquarters, 2901 W. Truman Blvd., Jefferson City, MO 65102; (573) 522-4115; http://mdc.mo.gov

Missouri Department of Natural Resources, PO Box 176, Jefferson City, MO 65102; (800) 361-4827; www.dnr.mo.gov

Missouri State Historic Sites, PO Box 176, Jefferson City, MO 65102; (800) 334-6946; http://mostateparks.com

Missouri State Parks, PO Box 176, Jefferson City, MO 65102; (800) 334-6946; http://mostateparks.com

Shawnee National Forest, 50 Highway 145 South, Harrisburg, IL 62946; (618) 253-7114; www.fs.usda.gov/shawnee

St. Louis County Parks, Recreation, and Forestry, 41 South Central, Clayton, MO 63105; (314) 615-4386; www.stlouisco.com/ParksandRecreation

It is important to keep in mind that from the time this book was published to the time that you are reading it, some land management rules and regulations may have already changed. You are encouraged to always check for new and updated information about the area you plan to visit.

*Rock formation along
the trail in Giant
City State Park*

How to Use This Guide

This guide is designed to be simple and easy to use. Each hike is described with a map and summary information that delivers the trail's vital statistics including length, difficulty, fees and permits, park hours, canine compatibility, and trail contacts. Directions to the trailhead are also provided, along with a general description of what you'll see along the way. A detailed route finder (Miles and Directions) sets forth mileages between significant landmarks along the trail.

Getting to the Trail

Most of the trails in this guide can be approached from one of the three major interstates that run through or out of St. Louis (I-55, I-64, and I-70) or by other major highways. Detailed directions from St. Louis to the trailheads are included in this guide. Google Maps (http://maps.google.com) provides excellent supplemental maps to aid you in finding your way.

How the Hikes Were Chosen

This guide describes trails that are accessible to almost every hiker, whether visiting from out of town or a local resident. The hikes are no longer than 13 miles round-trip, and most are considerably shorter. They range in difficulty from flat excursions perfect for a family outing to more challenging treks in the rolling hills of the Ozarks. While these trails are among the best, keep in mind that nearby trails, sometimes in the same park or sometimes in a neighboring open space, may offer options better suited to your needs. We've selected hikes in the immediate St. Louis metropolitan area, southern Illinois, and the northern Ozarks, so wherever your starting point, you'll find a great hike nearby.

Selecting a Hike

A variety of hikes are included in this guide. When selecting a hike, keep the goals and fitness level of you and those in your hiking party in mind. Do you want to just get out and enjoy nature? Do you want to get in a good workout? Do you want to immerse yourself in the history of the area? Figuring out what you hope to get out of a hike will help you when choosing your hiking destination. Also be aware of the goals of others in your hiking party. If you are hoping to log some serious trail miles and your partner is hoping to photograph spring wildflowers, neither of you is likely to accomplish your goal. When hiking with others it is a good idea to communicate individual goals before setting out for the hike.

It is also a good idea to keep individual fitness levels in mind when selecting a hike. You and those you choose to hike with will enjoy the trail more if you select a hike that is challenging, but not too challenging. All of the hikes in this guide have

Practice Leave No Trace—leave wildflowers for others to enjoy!

Mushroom on the forest floor

been assigned a difficulty rating. Accompanying that rating is the reasoning behind the rating. Carefully look at these ratings, along with overall mileage, when choosing a hike.

Easy hikes are generally short and relatively flat, taking no longer than an hour or two to complete.

Moderate hikes involve increased distance and relatively mild changes in elevation and will take two to three hours to complete.

Difficult hikes feature some steep stretches and often greater distances, and generally take longer than three hours to complete.

Keep in mind that what you think is easy is entirely dependent on your level of fitness and the adequacy of your gear (primarily shoes). Use the trail's length as a gauge of its relative difficulty—even if climbing is involved, it won't be too strenuous if the hike is less than 1 mile long. The Trail Finder lists "Best Hikes for Birders," "Best Hikes with Children," "Best Hikes with Dogs," "Best Hikes for Great Views," "Best Hikes for Nature Lovers," "Best Hikes for History Buffs," and "Best Hikes for Trail Runners." Use these categories as a jumping-off point when selecting a trail.

Approximate hiking times are based on the assumption that on flat ground, most walkers average 2 miles per hour. Adjust that rate by the steepness of the terrain and your level of fitness (subtract time if you're an aerobic animal or trail runner and add time if you're hiking with kids or photographers), and you have a ballpark hiking duration. Be sure to add more time if you plan to picnic or take part in other activities like bird watching, photography, or nature study.

Box turtle

Wildflower on Flint Quarry Trail (hike 14)

Trail Finder

Hike No.	Hike Name	Best Hikes for Birders	Best Hikes with Children	Best Hikes with Dogs	Best Hikes for Great Views	Best Hikes for Nature Lovers	Best Hikes for History Buffs	Best Hikes for Trail Runners
1	Forest Park Heels Path	●	●					
2	Cahokia Mounds Nature/Culture Trail	●	●				●	
3	Walkers Island Trail	●						
4	Goat Cliff Trail			●	●			●
5	Lone Spring Trail					●		
6	Graham Cave State Park Trails						●	
7	Busch Hiking and Biking Trail	●				●		
8	Lewis Trail			●	●			
9	Katy Trail: Weldon Spring to Matson						●	
10	Dogwood Trail	●				●		
11	Lime Kiln Trail	●				●		
12	Al Foster Trail		●					
13	Dogwood Ridge Trail via Losing Stream Trail					●		

Hike No.	Hike Name	Best Hikes for Birders	Best Hikes with Children	Best Hikes with Dogs	Best Hikes for Great Views	Best Hikes for Nature Lovers	Best Hikes for History Buffs	Best Hikes for Trail Runners
14	Flint Quarry Trail						●	
15	White Bison Trail		●				●	
16	River Scene Trail	●			●			●
17	Hickory Ridge Trail	●						
18	Spring Valley Trail			●				
19	Limestone Hill Trail		●				●	
20	Wilderness Trail					●		
21	Rockywood Trail						●	
22	1000 Steps Trail					●		
23	Mooner's Hollow Trail			●	●		●	
24	Devils Honeycomb Trail			●	●			
25	Scour Trail		●		●			
26	Ozark Trail: Taum Sauk Mountain State Park to Johnson's Shut-Ins State Park				●			

Hike No.	Hike Name	Best Hikes for Birders	Best Hikes with Children	Best Hikes with Dogs	Best Hikes for Great Views	Best Hikes for Nature Lovers	Best Hikes for History Buffs	Best Hikes for Trail Runners
27	Mina Sauk Falls Loop Trail / Ozark Trail to Devils Tollgate				●			
28	Trail through Time		●		●	●	●	
29	White Oaks Trail			●		●		●
30	Whispering Pines Trail—North Loop			●		●		
31	Sheppard Point Trail				●		●	
32	Lake Trail	●			●			
33	Pee–Wah Trail			●				●
34	Piney Creek Ravine Trail		●				●	
35	Waterfall Trail		●					
36	Pomona Natural Bridge		●					
37	Little Grand Canyon Trail				●	●		
38	Trillium Trail		●			●		
39	Giant City Nature Trail		●			●		●
40	Panther Den Trail		●			●		

Map Legend

Transportation

═🛡70🛡═	Freeway/Interstate Highway
═⬯50⬯═	US Highway
═⬯21⬯═	State Highway
═══════	Paved/Improved Road
══ ══ ══	Unpaved Road
+—+—+—+	Railroad

Trails

■■■■■■	Selected Route
- - - - - -	Trail
→	Direction of Route

Water Features

⬭	Body of Water
∿	River or Creek
╌╌╱╌╌	Intermittant Stream
≋	Waterfall
⌐	Spring

Symbols

🔵20	Trailhead
■	Building/Point of Interest
🅿	Parking
🚻	Restroom
🔷	Scenic View/Overlook
❓	Visitor Center/Information
⛱	Picnic Area
⛺	Campground
▲	Primitive Campsite
⏝	Bridge
⌒	Cave
◤	Boat Ramp
▲	Mountain/Peak
○	Towns and Cities

Land Management

▭	National Forest
▭	Wilderness Area
▭	State/Local Park

The Hikes

1 Forest Park Heels Path

Located in the heart of St. Louis and just off I-64, Forest Park is one of the largest urban parks in the United States. Owned and operated by the City of St. Louis, Forest Park is considered one of the city's most treasured resources. This easy, paved trail forms a loop around the perimeter of the park and passes several of the city's most popular attractions, including the St. Louis Science Center, the St. Louis Zoo, and the Missouri History Museum, all of which are available to the public free of charge.

Start: Dennis & Judith Jones Visitor and Education Center
Distance: 5.7-mile loop
Hiking time: 3 hours
Difficulty: Moderate due to length
Trail surface: Pavement and gravel
Best season: Year-round
Other trail users: Joggers and bikers
Canine compatibility: Leashed dogs permitted

Land status: Operated by City of St. Louis
Fees and permits: None
Maps: USGS Clayton; detailed trail map and brochure available at visitor center
Trail contact: Forest Park Forever, Dennis & Judith Jones Visitor and Education Center, 5595 Grand Dr., St. Louis, MO 63112; (314) 367-7275; www.forestparkforever.org

Finding the trailhead: From downtown St. Louis, take I-64 West / US 40 West to the exit for Kingshighway Boulevard. Take Kingshighway Boulevard north and turn left (west) onto Lindell Boulevard. Turn south (left) onto Cricket, and then turn right onto Grand Drive. The Dennis & Judith Jones Visitor and Education Center is ahead on the right. There is a large parking lot located across the street (south) from the visitor and education center. The trail begins on the north end of the visitor center. **GPS:** N38 38.604' / W90 16.957'

The Hike

Dedicated in 1876, the 1,371-acre Forest Park is one of the oldest and largest urban parks in the United States. Forest Park houses many attractions, including the zoo, art museum, history museum, Jewel Box, science center, and the Muny Theater. It also offers visitors an array of opportunities for outdoor activities, including tennis courts, a golf course, fishing, and the Steinberg skating rink. Hikers will enjoy the Forest Park Heels Path, which circles many of the park's best attractions.

With more than 18,000 trees, Forest Park provides ideal habitat for many species of birds, including five species of woodpeckers, several species of owls, and the iconic northern cardinal, which is the mascot for the city's baseball team. Other wildlife is also abundant in the park, and it is not uncommon for visitors to see squirrels, foxes, raccoons, muskrats, woodchucks, and chipmunks.

The trail begins at the north end of the Dennis & Judith Jones Visitor and Education Center. The visitor and education center offers water, restrooms, day lockers, and the Forest Park Cafe. It also houses Forest Park Forever, the nonprofit organization

Science playground

working to restore, maintain, and sustain Forest Park, and the Missouri Department of Conservation. Visitor information is provided through the St. Louis Convention and Visitors Commission.

From the north end of the Dennis & Judith Jones Visitor and Education Center, the trail turns to the right (east), following the northern border of the park. After 0.2 mile the trail crosses Cricket Drive and continues east, crossing Union Drive (0.5 mile) and Grand Drive (0.8 mile) before reaching Round Lake.

The path continues south, passing Jefferson Lake to the east. Jefferson Lake offers good fishing for St. Louis anglers. More than twenty-five species of fish can be found in Forest Park, including rainbow trout, largemouth bass, bluegill, channel catfish, and white crappie.

WORLD'S FAIR IN ST. LOUIS

The 1904 World's Fair, officially named the Louisiana Purchase Exhibition, was held in what is now Forest Park in St. Louis. The seven-month celebration included exhibits from sixty-two foreign nations. Food lovers can thank the fair for popularizing some of our favorite treats, including iced tea, hot dogs, and the waffle-style ice-cream cone.

River des Peres

At 1.0 mile there's a fork in the path—stay left to cross a bridge. At this point the walking path merges with the bike path and is shared by both users until the walking path reemerges near Tamm Avenue.

Cross Clayton Road at 1.5 miles and skirt around the James S. McDonnell Planetarium, which is connected to the St. Louis Science Center via a footbridge to the south. The St. Louis Science Center offers more than 700 exhibits, and general admission is free to the public.

FAMOUS REDHEADS

When most people think of a woodpecker, they picture the red-headed woodpecker. With its bright red head, blue-black back, and pure white belly, it is a striking bird. Forest Park provides important habitat for the red-headed woodpecker, which has seen a decline in population due to the loss of its breeding and nesting habitat. While visiting the park and other natural areas around St. Louis, look for dead and dying trees, which are favored by the woodpecker as nesting sites.

Forest Park Heels Path

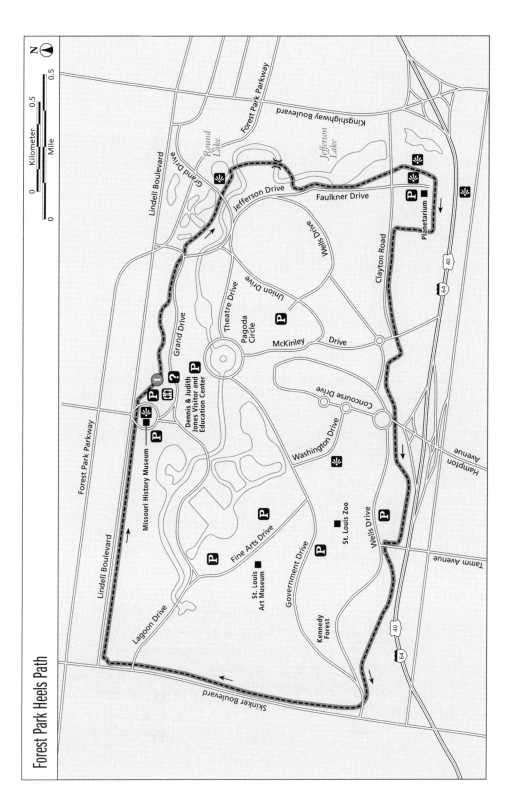

Pass the Science Playground and the Dinosaur Replicas at 1.6 miles. From here, the path turns to the right and follows the southern border of the park, crossing McKinley Drive (2.4 miles) and then traversing Hampton Avenue at Concourse Drive (2.7 miles) via a pedestrian underpass.

After traveling through the pedestrian underpass, the trail passes the St. Louis Zoo. Home to almost 23,000 animals from all over the world, the zoo offers free general admission and makes a fine addition to this hike. On the west end of the zoo parking lot, the trail crosses Tamm Avenue (3.3 miles).

At 3.8 miles cross Wells Drive and bear right (north) passing Kennedy Forest. After crossing Lagoon Drive (4.5 miles), the path curves to the right (east) to follow the northern border of the park. At 5.4 miles come to the Missouri History Museum, another great St. Louis resource that is available to the public free of charge. Just past the museum the trail veers to the southeast to complete the loop at the Dennis & Judith Jones Visitor and Education Center.

Miles and Directions

0.0 Begin at the Dennis & Judith Jones Visitor and Education Center and head east.

0.2 Cross Cricket Drive and continue east.

0.5 Cross Union Drive and continue on the walking trail as it bends to the right (southeast).

0.8 Cross Grand Drive and continue southeast, passing Round Lake to the left (north).

1.0 The walking path merges with a bike path. Where the trail forks, stay left and cross the bridge.

1.5 Cross Clayton Road and skirt around the James S. McDonnell Planetarium.

1.6 Pass the Science Playground and come to the Dinosaur Replicas.

2.4 Cross McKinley Drive and continue west.

2.7 Use the pedestrian underpass to traverse Hampton Avenue at Concourse Drive.

3.3 Cross Tamm Avenue and continue west on the walking path.

3.8 Cross Wells Drive and turn north.

4.5 Cross Lagoon Drive. Soon after, the trail curves to the right (east).

5.4 Reach the Missouri History Museum.

5.7 Arrive back at the Dennis & Judith Jones Visitor and Education Center.

GREEN TIP
Carpool, walk, ride your bike, or take public
transportation to the trailhead whenever possible.
This not only conserves resources but also cuts back on
overcrowding at popular trailheads.

2 Cahokia Mounds Nature/Culture Trail

This easy stroll explores the remains of the most sophisticated prehistoric Native American civilization north of Mexico. Once a center for trade and politics, Cahokia was even said to have been larger than London at the height of its existence. Even more intriguing is that this huge civilization seems to have vanished into thin air. Weaving its way around ancient mounds, this loop trail offers visitors an up-close look at the mysterious and ancient city known as Cahokia. Located just minutes from downtown St. Louis, Cahokia Mounds makes a fantastic day trip for hikers and history buffs alike.

Start: Northwest corner of visitor center
Distance: 4-mile loop
Hiking time: 2 hours
Difficulty: Easy due to flat terrain
Trail surface: Dirt, gravel, and grass
Best season: Fall through spring
Other trail users: None
Canine compatibility: Leashed dogs permitted

Land status: Operated by Illinois Department of Natural Resources
Fees and permits: None; small donation suggested
Maps: USGS Monks Mound; interpretive trail map available at visitor center
Trail contact: Cahokia Mounds State Historic Site, 30 Ramey St., Collinsville, IL 62234; (618) 346-5160; www.cahokiamounds.org

Finding the trailhead: From St. Louis, take I-55 North / I-70 East / US 40 East toward Illinois. After 6.7 miles exit toward IL 111 at exit 6 and turn right onto IL 111. Turn left after 0.2 mile onto Collinsville Road and drive 1.9 miles before turning right onto Ramey Street and arriving at the visitor center and trailhead parking. **GPS:** N38 39.309' / W90 3.574'

The Hike

The hike begins on the northwest corner of the visitor center, a great resource and a recommended stop for anyone wanting to learn about this unique historic site. The visitor center offers restrooms, water, vending machines, and a gift shop. It also houses a fantastic museum that informs visitors about the prehistoric Cahokia and brings to life the area through which you are about to hike. In the gift shop you can purchase or borrow an in-depth interpretive guide called the *Nature/Culture Hike Guidebook,* which describes the thirty-two markers you will see along this hike. The visitor center also allows guests to rent iPod Touch players for an audiovisual tour of three interpretive trails, another great resource.

This hike is all about seeing the famous "mounds" of Cahokia. There are more than one hundred mounds in the area, and this path will lead you past many of them. The mounds are made entirely of soil, which was transported by the people of Cahokia in baskets from around AD 700 to 1400. These mounds served several purposes for the Cahokians including their use as bases for ceremonial structures, location markers, and burial sites for important people of the time.

Monks Mound

You will encounter several impressive mounds on this hike. The first famous mound that you will come across is Mound 72 at 0.4 mile, which is the site of nearly 300 ceremonial and sacrificial burials. At 1.7 miles you will come to Woodhenge, a reconstructed sunrise horizon calendar. Constructed from cedar posts, the circular calendar is 410 feet in diameter and marked the seasons and important dates for the Cahokians. The largest mound you will encounter on this hike is Mound 38, also known as Monks Mound (2.7 miles), which is more than 100 feet tall and covers some 14 acres of land.

Despite being located in a heavily used area (I-55/70 and busy Collinsville Road cut across the site toward the northern border), the site is rich in natural history, and visitors are likely to encounter wildlife on the trail including the white-tailed deer, gray squirrel, red fox, and eastern chipmunk. Additionally, there are numerous examples of prairie grasses, flowering plants, and trees, many of which were staples in the everyday lives of the Cahokians.

DAMAGE TO THE MOUNDS

In the 1940s and 1950s, a subdivision of more than sixty houses was developed on a portion of the Cahokia Mounds site. The subdivision severely impacted several of the mounds found in the area and was eventually torn down in an attempt to preserve the cultural history at the site.

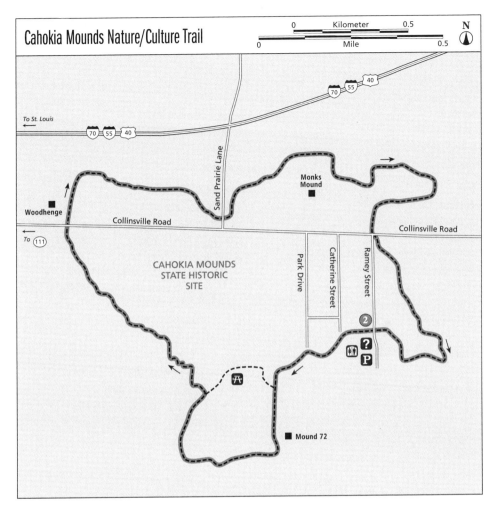

Cahokia Mounds Nature/Culture Trail

Miles and Directions

0.0 From the visitor center, follow the paved walkway to the left (southwest). The trail is marked with blue arrows.

0.4 Pass Mound 72 to the east and reach the end of the paved portion of the trail. Continue south, and then follow the blue arrows as the trail turns to the west, then north.

1.3 Avoid the spur trail branching to the right (marked with a white arrow), which returns to the visitor center. Stay left (northwest), following the blue arrow, to continue on the trail.

1.7 Cross Collinsville Road and continue north past Woodhenge.

2.3 Cross Sand Prairie Lane and continue east/northeast.

2.7 Come to the north end of Monks Mound and continue east.

3.4 Cross Collinsville Road again and continue south toward the visitor center.

3.9 Come to a connector trail, marked with a white arrow. Turn right (northwest) onto that trail to return to the visitor center.

4.0 Arrive back at the visitor center.

3 Walkers Island Trail

This easy and flat nature trail forms a loop around the perimeter of Walkers Island, which is located in a low floodplain that stretches as far south as Kentucky. Just minutes from downtown St. Louis, Walkers Island provides rich habitat for birds and other wildlife in the area and is a must-see for any birder. Walkers Island State Park allows picnicking, camping, and even hunting.

Start: North of trailhead parking area
Distance: 3.7-mile loop
Hiking time: 2 hours
Difficulty: Easy due to flat terrain
Trail surface: Grass and packed dirt
Best season: Year-round
Other trail users: None
Canine compatibility: Leashed dogs permitted

Land status: Operated by Illinois Department of Natural Resources
Fees and permits: None
Maps: USGS Monks Mound; interpretive trail map available at park office
Trail contact: Horseshoe Lake State Park, 3321 Highway 111, Granite City, IL 62040; (618) 931-0270, www.dnr.illinois.gov/parks/pages/horseshoelakemadison.aspx

Finding the trailhead: From St. Louis, take I-55 North / I-70 East / US 40 East toward Illinois. After 6.7 miles exit toward IL 111 at exit 6 and turn left onto IL 111. Continue for 3.1 miles until you reach the park entrance on the left. From the park entrance, follow the main road past the park office on the left and cross the causeway. At 0.8 mile from the entrance, reach the parking area and picnic shelter. The trailhead is located across the road (north) from the picnic shelter and parking area. **GPS:** N38 41.709' / W90 4.480'

The Hike

Despite being minutes from downtown St. Louis, Horseshoe Lake State Park feels far removed from city life. The park itself offers many recreational opportunities, including camping, hiking, hunting, fishing, and bird watching. Located in a low floodplain, Horseshoe Lake State Park provides perfect habitat for many species of wildlife. While the park is relatively small, you can expect to see several different types of habitats here.

Birds and other wildlife can find food and shelter on the lakeshore, in the hardwood woodland, near the marshy pond area, or in the agricultural land, all of which are located within the park. A birding checklist is provided at the park office and will clue hikers in on which birds they can expect to see on Walkers Island. Restrooms and water are available at the park office and at the campground.

The trail begins just north of the trailhead parking area. Follow the slightly worn path through the grass as it heads north toward the shore of Horseshoe Lake. The trailhead is marked with a sign indicating the start of the hiking trail. The obvious trail continues northeast following the shoreline. As you hike through this wooded section

Harwood Ponds

of the trail, you will notice many species of trees, including hackberry trees, which provide a valuable source of food for birds and wildlife.

After hiking 0.6 mile you'll come to an open area and the trail turns sharply to the left. This is the first watch area you will encounter on the hike and a great place to watch for wood ducks and other diving ducks that prefer the open water.

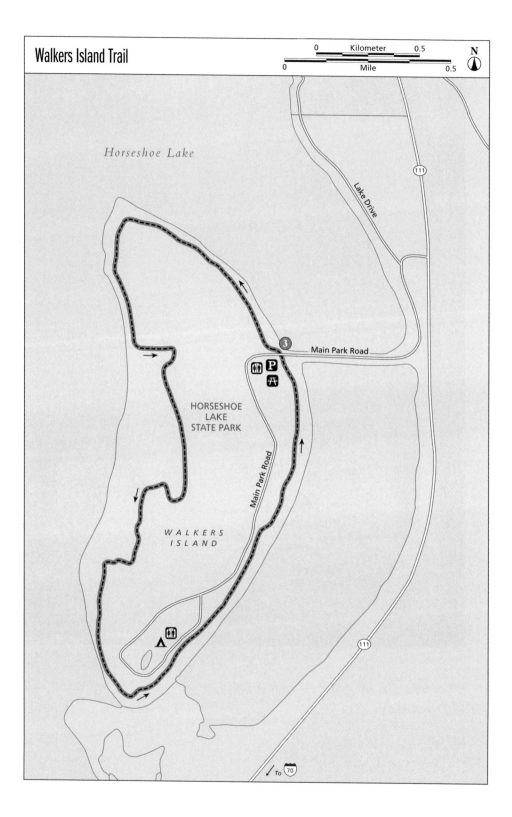

Walkers Island Trail

Horseshoe Lake

Lake Drive

111

Main Park Road

HORSESHOE
LAKE
STATE PARK

Main Park Road

WALKERS
ISLAND

111

To 70

Great white egret

The trail continues south, passing through old farm fields and, at 1.3 miles, the Hardwood Ponds, a "swampy" area with hardwood trees growing in and around the water. Keep an extra pair of dry shoes and socks in the car, as this area can be flooded from early to mid-spring. Both areas provide great habitat for wildlife. Look for white-tailed deer, coyotes, opossums, red foxes, box turtles, and beavers.

As you come to the southern end of the island, the trail curves to the left (east), passing through the campground (2.5 miles), and then returns to the trailhead and parking area via the eastern shore of the island.

Miles and Directions

0.0 From the trailhead parking area and picnic shelter, walk across the park road and follow the faint trail north as it heads toward the shore of Horseshoe Lake.

0.2 Reach the wooden hiking trail start sign.

0.6 The trail turns sharply to the left (south).

1.3 Pass through the Hardwood Ponds area.

2.5 Pass the campground on the left (west) and continue north, following the eastern shore of the island.

3.7 Arrive at the trailhead parking area and picnic shelter.

4 Goat Cliff Trail

Carved out by ancient glaciers and meltwaters, the Illinois River provides a picturesque backdrop for visitors to the area. Known for its abundant winter bald eagle population, Pere Marquette State Park has something for every type of outdoor enthusiast. This short but challenging hike offers some of the best views in the 8,000-acre park. Many visitors find the time to stop in the city of Grafton for a stroll around town.

Start: Northwest corner of parking area
Distance: 1.7-mile loop
Hiking time: 1 hour
Difficulty: Difficult due to demanding climb
Trail surface: Dirt packed trail
Best season: Spring through fall
Other trail users: None
Canine compatibility: Leashed dogs permitted

Land status: Operated by Illinois Department of Natural Resources
Fees and permits: None
Maps: USGS Brussels; park maps available at visitor center
Trail contact: Pere Marquette State Park, Route 100, PO Box 158, Grafton, IL 62037; (618) 786-3323; www.dnr.illinois.gov/parks/pages/peremarquette.aspx

Finding the trailhead: From downtown St. Louis, take I-70 West to Goodfellow Boulevard at exit 242. Turn right (east) on Goodfellow Boulevard for 2.3 miles to a roundabout, then turn onto 367 North / Lewis & Clark Boulevard. Take 367 North / Lewis & Clark Boulevard / 67 North for 13.4 miles into Illinois and bear left onto 67 North / Landmarks Boulevard / Great River Road for 0.9 mile to the intersection with IL 100. Turn left onto IL 100 and continue for 8.6 miles, at which point the road becomes US 67 North and continues for 20.9 miles to the Pere Marquette State Park entrance. Continue 0.5 mile from the park entrance on IL 100 before turning right onto Scenic Drive and then left into the visitor center and trailhead parking area. The trailhead is located on the northwest corner of the parking area. **GPS:** N38 58.413'/ W90 32.660'

The Hike

Except for the hottest of summer days, Pere Marquette State Park is a pleasant trip for outdoor enthusiasts looking for great camping, hiking, biking, horseback riding, fishing, and bird watching. During the fall visitors are treated to an array of colors as the leaves change. Throughout the winter months it is common to see the bald eagles that make their winter home along the Illinois River. Wildflowers and wildlife are in abundance in springtime. Even summer can be a pleasant time to visit, since much of the park enjoys the shaded cover of the woodland canopy.

While Pere Marquette State Park offers several great hiking trails, the Goat Cliff Trail is perhaps the most scenic and makes a great place to begin your explorations in the park.

From the northwest corner of the parking area, locate the obvious dirt trail heading north. Follow this trail as it briefly parallels IL 100 before it begins to ascend a

View of Illinois River from the Goat Cliff Hill Prairie Overlook

moderate ridge. At 0.2 mile you'll arrive at Twin Springs. Notice the oddly angled rocks that represent the Cap au Gres Fault. Take a moment to appreciate the fact that you are standing on a fault line, then continue north through the mixed woodland of sugar maples, oaks, and hickories. At 0.7 mile come to a scenic overlook, which offers a good view of the farm valley to the northwest.

Cap au Gres Fault

BALD EAGLES

A national symbol of the United States since 1782, the bald eagle can be found throughout much of North America, particularly near water. It is most common in Alaska, parts of Florida, and, during the winter months, parts of the Midwest. Placed on the national endangered species list in the 1970s, the bald eagle has made a gradual comeback in many areas thanks to conservation programs and the banning of harmful pesticides. Its nest, known as an aerie, is composed of sticks and located up to 150 feet above the ground, usually in a tall tree near water. The aerie is renovated and added to every year, increasing in size until either its own weight or a winter storm destroys it. Eggs are incubated by both parents for about thirty-five days, and the chicks, known as eaglets, leave the nest just ten weeks after they have hatched. Live eagle cams have become popular in recent years and folks interested in the Pere Marquette eagles should check with the visitor center for updates on the park's eagle cam status.

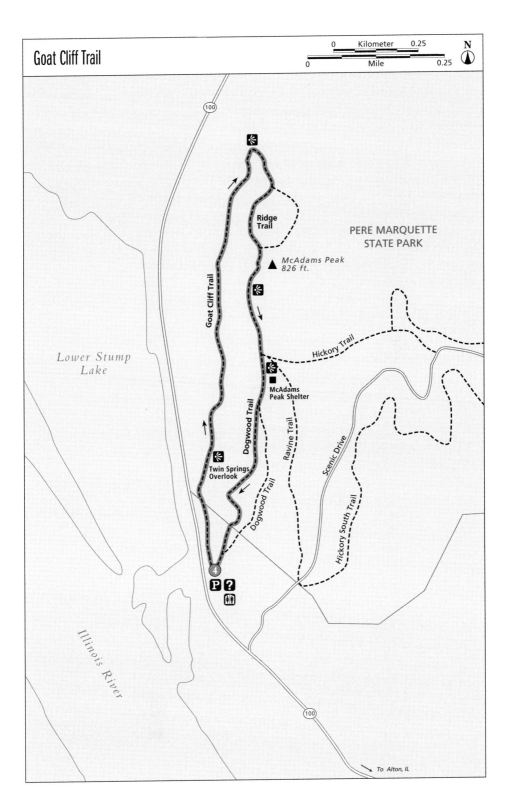

Goat Cliff Trail

0   Kilometer   0.25

0   Mile   0.25

N

100

Ridge Trail

PERE MARQUETTE STATE PARK

▲ McAdams Peak
826 ft.

Goat Cliff Trail

Lower Stump Lake

Hickory Trail

McAdams Peak Shelter

Dogwood Trail

Ravine Trail

Scenic Drive

Twin Springs Overlook

Dogwood Trail

Hickory South Trail

4

P ? 🚻

Illinois River

100

To Alton, IL

From the overlook, the trail turns to the southeast and follows the backside of the ridgeline. At 0.9 mile you'll come to a fork in the trail and bear right onto the smaller trail to visit the Goat Cliff Hill Prairie Overlook, which is part of the McAdams Peak Hill Prairie Natural Area. The trail rejoins the Goat Cliff Trail at 1.0 mile, just before the McAdams Peak Shelter, which offers another pretty place to take in the views of the Illinois River.

Several trails converge at McAdams Peak Shelter, and hikers wishing to extend their trip can follow the Hickory Trail east, which links to several other longer trails. The visitor center offers a trail map that lists all the trails within the park and should be consulted before extending this hike. The most direct route back to the trailhead parking area is the Ridge Trail, which heads south from McAdams Peak Shelter for 0.2 mile until it converges with the Dogwood Trail at 1.3 miles. You can follow either leg of the Dogwood Trail back to the trailhead parking area, but the leg that forks to the right (southwest) offers a final scenic overlook. At 1.5 miles turn right (south) and come to the trailhead parking area at 1.7 miles.

Miles and Directions

0.0 From the trailhead, follow the obvious path northeast.

0.2 Come to Twin Springs and the Cap au Gres Fault and continue north.

0.7 Reach a scenic overlook and follow the trail as it turns sharply to the south.

0.9 Bear right (southwest) at the fork in the trail and take the small side trail to Goat Cliff Hill Prairie Overlook.

1.0 The side trail rejoins Goat Cliff Trail. Continue south on the Goat Cliff Trail.

1.1 Come to McAdams Peak Shelter and continue south on the Ridge Trail.

1.3 Come to the Dogwood Trail and bear right (southwest).

1.5 Turn right (south) toward the parking area.

1.7 Arrive back at the trailhead / visitor center parking area.

5 Lone Spring Trail

Located in Cuivre River State Park, the Lone Spring Trail provides an interesting trek through a dense woodland of white oak, black oak, shagbark hickory, and northern red oak. Lone Spring appears from under a shelf of limestone and offers hikers a calm spot to relax and take in the sights and sounds of this unique park. The park offers numerous recreational opportunities. In addition to the park's eleven hiking trails, visitors can stay in the campground, boat, swim, fish, or just relax and enjoy the Ozark-like topography.

Start: Lone Spring Trail parking area
Distance: 5.8-mile lollipop
Hiking time: 3 hours
Difficulty: Difficult due to length
Trail surface: Packed dirt and gravel
Best season: Spring through fall
Other trail users: None
Canine compatibility: Leashed dogs permitted

Land status: Operated by Missouri State Parks
Fees and permits: None
Maps: USGS Okete; park map available at visitor center
Trail contact: Cuivre River State Park, 678 State Route 147, Troy, MO 63379; (636) 528-7247; http://mostateparks.com/cuivre.htm

Finding the trailhead: From St. Louis, take I-64 West / US 40 West for about 40 miles until the road becomes US 61 North. Continue on US 61 North for 14.8 miles. Take the MO 47 ramp toward Troy and turn right onto MO 47. Drive 3.1 miles and turn left onto MO 147. Continue on MO 147 for 1.8 miles to the visitor center. At the visitor center turn right onto Lincoln Hills Road and drive 5 miles through the park until the road meets Highway KK. The parking area is to the right and the trailhead is located across KK. **GPS:** N39 3.948' / W90 55.997'

The Hike

Located northwest of St. Louis, Cuivre River State Park stands in contrast to other natural areas located in northern Missouri. Its landscape is comparable in many ways to that of the Ozarks, and the caves, springs, sinkholes, rocky creeks, and dramatic limestone bluffs found here make it a worthy destination for any hiker. The visitor center offers displays on the area's cultural and natural history, as well as restrooms, water, and park maps.

Hikers visiting in warmer months will enjoy cooling off in Lake Lincoln, a 55-acre man-made lake that is open for swimming (closed to boats with gas motors) and features a sandy public beach. Hikers may also want to make time to explore the gravel bars, limestone bluffs, and small swimming holes in the Big Sugar Creek Natural Area.

From the trailhead parking area, cross Highway KK and locate the Lone Spring Trail about 30 yards to the left (northwest). A sign alerts visitors that they are entering the Northwoods Wild Area and a smaller sign marks the beginning of the Lone

Spiderwort along Lone Spring Trail

Spring Trail. Enter the woods here and turn left (west) onto the Lone Spring Trail. After 0.3 mile reach the trailhead register. Sign in and turn right (northwest) to continue on the Lone Spring Trail.

At 1.3 miles come to a spur trail, which forks left and leads to Lone Spring and a wooden bench, offering hikers an ideal place to relax. After taking in the sights of Lone Spring, follow the spur trail back to the Lone Spring Trail and continue northeast, passing a sinkhole on the right. Avoid the spur trail at 1.6 miles, which leads to a backcountry campsite, and follow the yellow arrow northeast to continue on the Lone Spring Trail.

Reach a spur trail at 2.5 miles, which heads north for 0.5 mile to Shady 80 Lake and offers a nice side trip and primitive camping options. At 3.0 miles cross Highway KK and continue on to the Lone Spring Trail—South Loop. The trail branching to the west leads back to the trailhead parking area and will shorten your hike. Enter a grove of eastern cedars after 4.0 miles and shortly after that cross Lincoln Hills Road and follow the trail as it turns to the northwest.

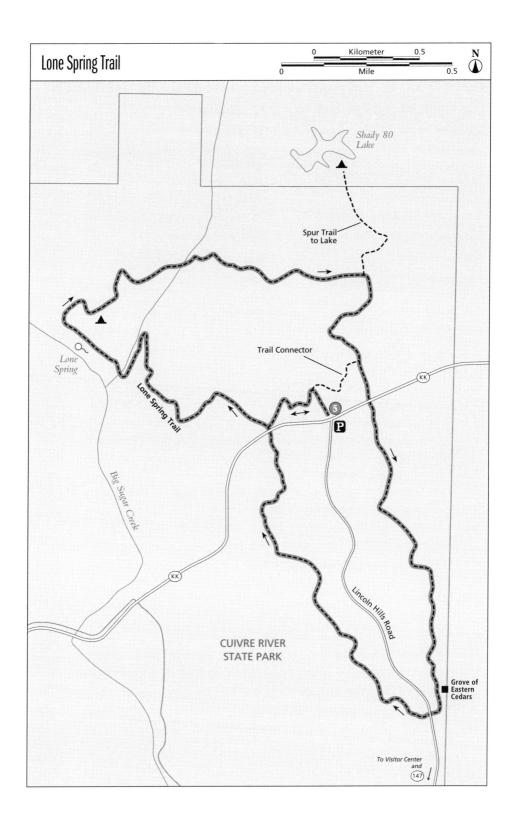

Lone Spring Trail

Kilometer

0   0.5

Mile

0   0.5

N

Shady 80 Lake

Spur Trail to Lake

Trail Connector

Lone Spring

Lone Spring Trail

KK

5

P

Big Sugar Creek

KK

Lincoln Hills Road

CUIVRE RIVER STATE PARK

Grove of Eastern Cedars

To Visitor Center and

147

MORE TRAILS IN CUIVRE RIVER STATE PARK

Cuivre River State Park offers some of the finest day hikes in Missouri. The Lone Spring Trail is our favorite, but if you live in the St. Louis area or visit the area often, you will not be disappointed by the park's other trails. Here is a list of trails in the park, in order of length, that you may want to check out on your own. Stop by the park's visitor center for more information on these hikes.

Prairie Trail, 0.3 mile

Mossy Hill Trail, 0.8 mile

Turkey Hollow Trail, 0.8 mile

Hamilton Hollow Trail, 0.9 mile

Frenchman's Bluff Trail, 1.25 miles

Blazing Star Trail, 2.0 miles

Lakeside Trail, 3.5 miles

Big Sugar Creek Trail, 3.75 miles

Blackhawk Point Trail, 5.75 miles

Cuivre River Trail, 11.25 miles

After 5.3 miles cross Highway KK for the final time. Follow the trail into the woods and turn right (east) at the trailhead register, following the trail back to the trailhead parking area.

Miles and Directions

0.0 From the trailhead, enter the woods and turn left (west) onto the Lone Spring Trail.

0.3 Come to the trailhead register. Turn right (northwest) to continue on the Lone Spring Trail.

1.3 Come to a spur trail branching to the left. Go left to visit Lone Spring or stay right to continue on the Lone Spring Trail.

1.6 Avoid the spur trail leading to the backcountry camping area.

2.5 Come to the spur trail, branching to the north, for Shady 80 Lake.

3.0 Continue southeast and cross Highway KK.

4.0 Enter the grove of eastern cedars.

4.1 Cross Lincoln Hills Road and continue on the trail as it turns to the northwest.

5.3 Cross Highway KK, follow the trail into the woods, and turn right (east) at the trailhead register.

5.8 Arrive back at the trailhead.

GREEN TIP
Reduce the amount of trash you take into the wilderness
by removing extra packaging from food items or by repacking food
into reusable ziplock bags before you leave home.
This practice minimizes the potential for small pieces of trash
to be dropped or carried off by the wind.

6 Graham Cave State Park Trails

Graham Cave State Park is located just off of I-70, west of St. Louis. A series of trails within the park make up a 3-mile loop highlighted by Graham Cave. The hike itself is a moderate stroll through a moist bottomland forest, a rocky oak-hickory forest, sandstone glades, and dolomite glades. Be sure to make a pit stop at the visitor center as you first enter the park.

Start: West end of parking area
Distance: 3-mile loop
Hiking time: 2 hours
Difficulty: Moderate
Trail surface: Dirt packed trail, gravel, and pavement
Best seasons: Spring and fall
Other trail users: None
Canine compatibility: Leashed dogs permitted

Land status: Operated by Missouri State Parks
Fees and permits: None
Maps: USGS Montgomery City; trail maps available at park office / visitor center
Trail contact: Graham Cave State Park, 217 Highway TT, Danville, MO 63361; (573) 564-3476; https://mostateparks.com/park/graham-cave-state-park

Finding the trailhead: From St. Louis, take I-64 West / US 40 West for 40 miles to I-70 West. Merge left onto I-70 West and continue for 40 miles to exit 170. Turn right onto MO 161 and then take an immediate left onto Highway TT. Drive 2.6 miles on Highway TT into Graham State Park to the Loutre River trailhead. **GPS:** N38 54.186' / W91 34.603'

The Hike

Graham Cave was the first archaeological site in the United States to be designated a National Historic Landmark. Artifacts uncovered in the cave that dated back to the Dalton and Archaic periods (as early as 10,000 years ago) showed archaeologists that the Native Americans who lived here depended mainly on hunting and fishing for survival. The cave became a National Historic Landmark in 1961, the land became a state park in 1964, and more excavations of the cave were done in 1966.

The cave is the highlighted feature of the park. It is formed of dolomite and sandstone and extends almost 100 feet into the hill where it sits. The arch-like opening of the cave is 16 feet high and 120 feet wide.

This park boasts 356 acres to explore, including 82 acres of Graham Cave Glades Natural Area. The park offers picnic sites, playgrounds, interpretive sites, a campground (primitive and electric sites and hot showers), river access, and hiking trails. A series of short trails connect to create a loop that takes visitors from a stroll along the Loutre River to an oak-hickory forest and through the glades.

After stopping at the park office just after entering the park, continue on Highway TT until it ends in a large parking area. Locate the Loutre River trailhead at the

Graham Cave

GRAHAM CAVE HISTORY

Formed at the contact point of Jefferson City dolomite and St. Peter sandstone, Graham Cave was created by the persisting actions of both water and wind. The large, arching entrance measures 120 feet wide and 16 feet high and gives visitors a glimpse into the cave's unusual history.

The property on which the cave sits was purchased from Daniel Morgan Boone, son of the famous Daniel Boone, in 1847 by Robert Graham. D. F. Graham, son of Robert, originally used the cave as a shelter for his hogs but soon discovered that it held a wealth of archaeological artifacts. After the Graham family donated many of the artifacts to the University of Missouri, interest in the cave expanded, and its archaeological potential was initially assessed in 1930.

A more extensive study, conducted by the University of Missouri and the Missouri Archaeological Society, took place from 1949 to 1955. During this excavation researchers, using carbon dating, found evidence that man had used the cave for nearly 10,000 years. Artifacts in this cave provided archaeologists with clues about humans' adaptations to the environment around the end of the Pleistocene Ice Age.

Due to the significant archaeological findings, in 1961 Graham Cave became the first archaeological site in the United States to be designated a National Historic Landmark. The cave was later placed on the National Register of Historic Places.

It remained in the Graham family until its transfer to the state in 1964.

Footbridge in Graham Cave State Park

westernmost end of the parking lot. Begin hiking west on the Loutre River Trail until you reach a park road at 0.3 mile. The trail follows the road southwest and then leaves the road, turning right (northwest) at 0.5 mile. At 0.6 mile you'll stay left to avoid the return loop for the Loutre River Trail and then avoid another trail (white connector), staying left at 0.8 mile.

Graham Cave State Park Trails

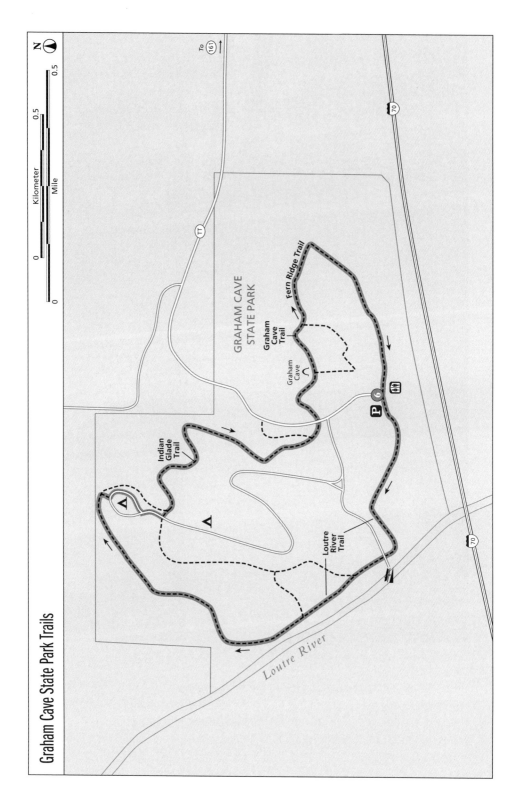

After 1.4 miles the trail opens up into the park campground. Hike southwest through the campground and turn left (southeast) onto the Indian Glade Trail at 1.6 miles. Continue on the Indian Glade Trail past the Woodland Way Trail access at 2.2 miles and cross the park road on the way to Graham Cave at 2.5 miles. Hike east from Graham Cave onto the Graham Cave Trail and then continue northeast at 2.6 miles onto the Fern Ridge Trail. Follow the Fern Ridge Trail for another 0.4 mile to the east end of the parking area and return to the Loutre River trailhead.

Miles and Directions

0.0 From the west end of the Loutre River parking area, locate the Loutre River trailhead and begin hiking west.

0.3 The trail turns left (southwest) and parallels the park road.

0.5 Turn right (northwest) to stay on the trail.

0.6 Stay left. The trail to the right is the return trail for the Loutre River Trail.

0.8 Avoid the connector trail on the right.

1.4 The trail reaches the campground. Turn right (south) and hike through the campground along the park road.

1.6 Turn left (southeast) onto the Indian Glade Trail.

2.2 Avoid the Woodland Way Trail on the left and cross the park road to continue on the Indian Glade Trail.

2.5 Reach Graham Cave and continue hiking east onto the Graham Cave Trail.

2.6 Come to a Y and go left onto the Fern Ridge Trail.

3.0 Arrive at the east side of the parking area.

GREEN TIP

There are more than 6,000 caves in Missouri. Many of these caves provide habitat for a variety of bat species. In 2010 ecologists found bats in Missouri that had a disease commonly referred to as "white-nose syndrome." While not thought to be dangerous to humans or other animals, this disease has killed more than a million bats in the United States since 2006. Several caves have been closed in Missouri to help protect the spread of this disease. Please be mindful of these closures, and if you come to a cave where there are no posted signs, please check with local land managers before entering the cave.

7 Busch Hiking and Biking Trail

The August A. Busch Memorial Conservation Area is well known to locals for its thirty-two fishable lakes and ponds, which provide habitat for bass, catfish, crappie, sunfish, and trout. The nearly 7,000 acres also provide quality flat-terrain hiking for anyone looking for a leisurely stroll. Other activities include bird watching, bicycling, hunting, and wildlife viewing. Pick up your fishing permits at the visitor center when you first enter the conservation area. A gift shop, snack stand, restrooms, and interpretive center are located at the visitor center as well.

Start: Busch Hiking Trail trailhead
Distance: 3.2-mile double loop
Hiking time: 2 hours
Difficulty: Easy due to flat terrain
Trail surface: Dirt packed trail and grass
Best season: Year-round
Other trail users: Bikers
Canine compatibility: Leashed dogs permitted
Land status: Operated by Missouri Department of Conservation

Fees and permits: None
Maps: USGS Defiance; detailed area map available at visitor center
Trail contact: August A. Busch Memorial Conservation Area, 2360 Highway D, St. Charles, MO 63304; (636) 441-4554; https://nature.mdc.mo.gov/discover-nature/places/busch-august-mem-ca

Finding the trailhead: From St. Louis, take I-64 West/US 40 West for almost 29 miles to exit 10. Turn left onto MO 94 and proceed 1.2 miles to Highway D. Turn right onto Highway D and drive 2 miles before turning right into the conservation area. After 0.2 mile turn left and drive 0.6 mile on the unnamed park road. Turn right after Lake 1 and drive 1.6 miles on the dirt road to the Busch Hiking and Biking Trail. **GPS:** N38 43.621'/W90 46.011'

The Hike

The August A. Busch Memorial Conservation Area is made up of 6,987 acres, 3,000 of which are forest. The remaining acreage is made up of grassland, wetland, prairies, and lakes. The area offers hiking, fishing, shooting ranges, boat rentals, picnicking, a visitor center, and more. It's hard to believe that an area offering so much was actually used to test TNT by the army in the 1940s and was even used for uranium ore processing in the 1960s. A massive federal environmental cleanup was conducted in the 1970s and 1980s to ensure that the area is safe for use.

The Busch Hiking Trail is a perfect opportunity for novice hikers and families to introduce themselves to numerous wonders of nature. The trail itself is easy to follow, consists of two loops, and covers very flat terrain. Be ready to see plenty of songbirds, quails, hawks, and deer. If you're lucky, you might see owls, coyotes, and/or beavers. Several old TNT bunkers can be seen from the trail, and the larger loop circles around two fishing lakes. Bring your fishing pole—the lakes are stocked with

TNT storage bunker in August A. Busch Memorial Conservation Area

bluegill, crappie, bass, catfish, and more. A fishing permit can be purchased at the visitor center for a small fee.

After entering the conservation area and turning right to check out the visitor center, make your way to the Busch Hiking Trail. From the trailhead, begin hiking northwest on the mostly grassy trail. Pass a few old TNT bunkers along the way and

TEN BIRDS TO LOOK FOR ON THE BUSCH HIKING AND BIKING TRAIL

The August A. Busch Memorial Conservation Area provides important habitat for birds in the St. Louis area. Here are ten birds to keep an eye out for while hiking:

1. Bald eagle
2. Wood duck
3. Osprey
4. Great horned owl
5. Red-headed woodpecker

6. Ruby-throated hummingbird
7. Green heron
8. Northern shrike
9. Great egret
10. Black-billed cuckoo

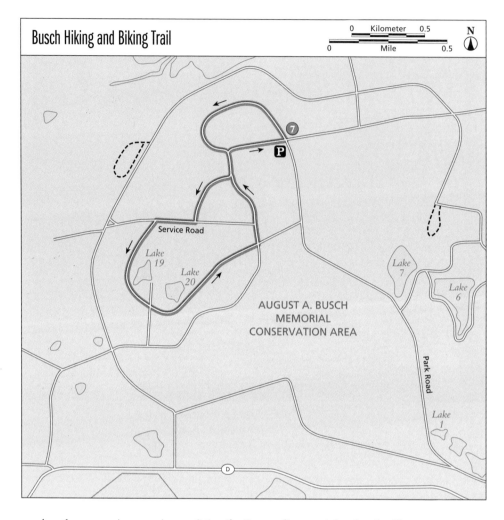

reach a three-way intersection at 0.6 mile. Proceeding straight ahead will return you to the trailhead—instead, turn right (south) to continue to the larger loop. At 0.8 mile you will reach another three-way intersection. Turn right (west) and continue on. Reach a service road at 1.0 mile and turn right (west) as the trail follows the road for a short distance. At 1.2 miles turn left (south) as the trail leaves the service road and continues toward Lake 19.

You can catch views of Lake 19 at 1.4 miles and gain access to Lakes 19 and 20 at 1.6 miles (by turning left), where the hiking trail turns right (south) to follow an access road for a short distance. At 1.8 miles the trail leaves the access road turning left (east). Continue on the trail until it reaches another access road at 2.5 miles and keep hiking north on the trail. After 2.8 miles complete the large loop and bear right (north) before reaching the final intersection at 2.9 miles. Turn right (east) and return to the trailhead at 3.2 miles.

Miles and Directions

0.0 From the Busch Hiking Trail trailhead, begin hiking northwest.

0.6 Reach an intersection and turn right (south).

0.8 Reach another intersection and turn right (west).

1.0 The trail turns right (west) and follows a service road.

1.2 The trail leaves the service road and continues southwest.

1.6 The trail follows an access road south for 0.2 mile.

1.8 Turn left (east) to continue on the Busch Hiking Trail.

2.5 The trail crosses an access road. Continue north.

2.8 Stay right (north) at the intersection.

2.9 Come to a second intersection and turn right (east).

3.2 Arrive back at the trailhead.

GREEN TIP

Q. Do you know what the most commonly found pieces of litter are near fishing areas?

A. Fishing line and bait cups

Issue: Other than the fact that it is not attractive to look at, animals can become tangled in the fishing line. The pungent smell of bait cups can attract animals and pests to the area, which is unhealthy for both anglers and animals.

8 Lewis Trail

This loop hike takes you through the Weldon Spring Conservation Area. Towering limestone bluffs offering excellent views of the Missouri River, an abundance of wildlife, and easy access from St. Louis combine to make for an ideal day trip.

Start: Eastern end of parking area
Distance: 8-mile loop
Hiking time: 4 hours
Difficulty: Difficult due to length and demanding climbs
Trail surface: Dirt packed trail
Best season: Fall through spring
Other trail users: None
Canine compatibility: Leashed dogs permitted

Land status: Operated by Missouri Department of Conservation
Fees and permits: None
Maps: USGS Weldon Spring; park map and brochure available at visitor center
Trail contact: Missouri Department of Conservation, St. Louis Regional Office, 2360 Highway D, St. Charles, MO 63304; (636) 441-4554; http://mdc7.mdc.mo.gov/applications/mo atlas/AreaSummaryPage.aspx?txtAreaID=7404

Finding the trailhead: From St. Louis, drive almost 29 miles on I-64 West / US 40 West to MO 94 West at exit 10. Turn left onto MO 94 and drive 2.4 miles to the Weldon Spring Conservation Area parking and Lewis and Clark trailheads. **GPS:** N38 41.445' / W90 43.452'

The Hike

Located in St. Charles County, the 8,359-acre Weldon Spring Conservation Area offers a variety of natural features, including large plots of forest, tall limestone bluffs, wetlands, glades, pastures, and some agricultural land. This combination of habitats makes for a diverse collection of flora and fauna in the area, despite its close proximity to the city. Weldon Spring once housed a World War II munitions plant, but visitors today are much more likely to see the area's abundance of plants and wildlife. White-tailed deer, wild turkeys, raccoons, squirrels, foxes, and five-lined skinks (a type of lizard) are just some of the wild animals that flourish here. The southern border of the area is formed by the Missouri River. The Katy Trail, a 240-mile biking-and-walking trail, cuts across the southern portion of Weldon Spring Conservation Area.

Located next to the information kiosk, the Lewis and the Clark Trails begin at the eastern end of the parking area. The trailhead is marked with a wooden sign that reads "Clark Trail 5.3 Miles" and "Lewis Trail 8.2 Miles." Begin hiking north on the obvious path, passing eastern red cedar, roughleaf dogwood, honey locust, and eastern redbud trees. After 0.1 mile the trail forks. Stay right (south), following the white arrow.

At 1.3 miles you gain sight of the Missouri River and come to an interpretive sign, which provides historical information on the Lewis and Clark expedition. Follow the trail as it turns sharply to the left (north).

View of Missouri River

After climbing a moderately steep ridge, pass one of several scenic overlooks at 2.2 miles. The impressive limestone bluffs tower above the Missouri River and the famous Katy Trail. From here the trail descends the ridge to a dry creek bottom (2.8 miles). Cross the creek and follow its bank to the intersection of the Clark Trail and the Lewis Trail. Stay right (east) to continue on the Lewis Trail.

GREEN TIP

We love hiking with our pets! It's great exercise, and dogs are arguably the best hiking partners—they never complain and they are always ready to thoroughly explore a new trail.

If you choose to hike with your pet, please be a responsible pet owner. You can do this by always cleaning up after your pet and keeping pets under control at all times. Pet waste is smelly, unsightly, and a health hazard for both humans and wildlife. Keeping your pet on a leash or under voice control is the best way to ensure that your pet is safe and not a nuisance to other hikers or wildlife. By doing these two simple things, you are doing your part to ensure that trails remain open to both you and your four-legged friends.

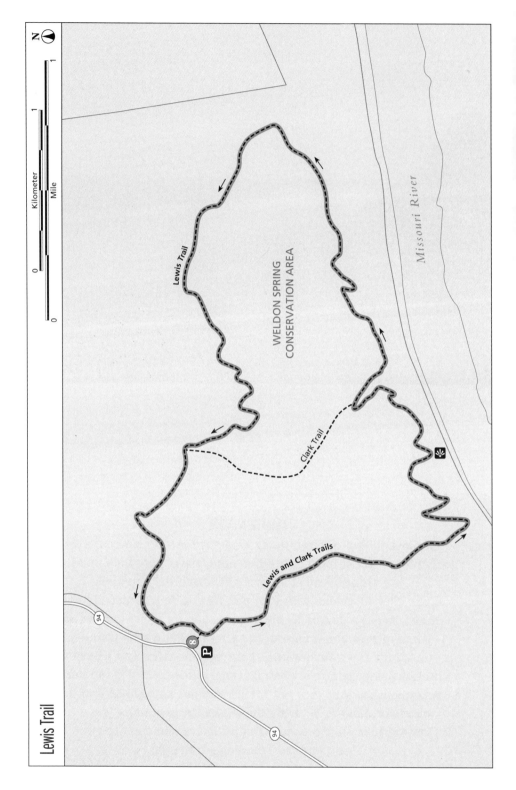

Lewis Trail

Lewis Trail through the forest

The trail follows an old fence line (3.3 miles) along the bluffs, before descending again via a series of mellow switchbacks through a mostly maple-and-oak forest. The trail crosses a small footbridge at 5.4 miles and then an access road at 5.6 miles.

At 6.4 miles the trail rejoins the Clark Trail. Stay right (north) at this intersection to complete the loop. Cross another footbridge at 7.0 miles and continue southwest to the trailhead parking area.

Miles and Directions

0.0   From the trailhead, begin hiking southeast on the combined Lewis and Clark Trails.

0.1   Come to a fork; turn right (south) to stay on the Lewis and Clark Trails.

1.3   Arrive at the Lewis and Clark interpretive sign and follow the trail as it curves to the left (north).

2.2   After ascending a moderately steep ridge, come to a series of overlooks.

2.8   Cross a dry creek bottom. Stay right to continue on the Lewis Trail. (*Option:* Follow the Clark Trail to the left for a shorter hike totaling 5.3 miles. You'll rejoin the Lewis Trail in 0.9 mile by turning left [northwest] and following the combined trail back to the trailhead. See mile point 6.4 below.)

3.3   Follow the trail as it parallels an old fence line along limestone bluffs.

5.4   Cross a small footbridge.

5.6   Cross an access road.

6.4   At the intersection with the Clark Trail, stay right (north) to complete the loop.

7.0   Cross a footbridge and continue southwest.

8.0   Arrive back at the trailhead parking area.

9 Katy Trail: Weldon Spring to Matson

The Katy Trail is the longest developed rail-trail in the United States. Running from Clinton to Machens, Missouri, the 240-mile trail stretches across almost the entire width of the state and is popular with runners, hikers, and bikers alike. The portion of trail between the Weldon Spring and Matson trailheads is a particularly beautiful stretch and makes a fine day hike and a short trip from St. Louis. Plan for a stop in the town of Defiance, a popular destination for lunch or ice cream.

Start: Trailhead parking area
Distance: 9.2 miles out and back
Hiking time: 4 hours
Difficulty: Easy due to flat terrain
Trail surface: Gravel
Best season: Year-round
Other trail users: Bikers and runners
Canine compatibility: Leashed dogs permitted

Land status: Operated by Missouri State Parks
Fees and permits: None
Maps: USGS Weldon Spring; trail maps located at Weldon Spring trailhead
Trail contact: Katy Trail State Park, 5901 S. Highway 163, Columbia, MO 65203; (573) 449-7402; https://mostateparks.com/park/katy-trail-state-park

Finding the trailhead: From St. Louis, take I-64 West / US 40 West for almost 29 miles to exit 10. Turn left onto MO 94 and continue for 5.3 miles to the Weldon Spring access for the Katy Trail, located on the left. Turn left and drive 0.3 mile to the parking area. **GPS:** N38 39.603' / W90 44.663'

The Hike

The Katy Trail is one of the premier destinations for outdoor adventure in Missouri. Bicyclists, hikers, nature lovers, and history buffs flock to the 240-mile trail. Once a corridor for the Missouri-Kansas-Texas (MKT) Railroad, the trail currently stretches from St. Charles to Clinton, Missouri, with plans for an additional section to be added between St. Charles and Machens, Missouri.

Closely following the Missouri River, the trail provides access to some of the most scenic areas in the state. With twenty-five trailheads, the Katy Trail offers recreationalists a plethora of hiking and biking options. Whether you spend two hours or two weeks on the trail, you will be pleased by both the natural and cultural history of the areas that the trail passes through.

Located just minutes from St. Louis, the Katy Trail from Weldon Spring to Matson offers a wonderful day trip for hikers looking to escape the city. This scenic section passes through the Weldon Spring Wildlife Area. You will pass towering limestone bluffs as the trail follows the Missouri River west through the historic town of Defiance to the small town of Matson.

View of Defiance, Missouri, from the Katy Trail

From the trailhead parking area, walk north to the restrooms and information kiosk. Follow the obvious gravel trail west toward the towns of Defiance and Matson. At 0.6 mile come to the intersection with the Hamburg Trail, which leads north to the Weldon Spring Interpretive Center and the August A. Busch Wildlife Area. Continue traveling west on the Katy Trail, leaving the Weldon Spring Wildlife Area at 0.9 mile.

At 1.3 miles follow the trail across the train truss over Femme Osage Creek. Cross Darst Bottom Road at 2.2 miles. At 2.9 miles the trees become less dense and you will gain views of the historic and idyllic town of Defiance. While this is not a strenuous hike, Defiance does offer several options for lodging, food, and beverages, as well as some interesting shops, which make for a fun detour from your trip or a great place to refuel after your hike.

At 3.8 miles the trail comes to MO 94. Use caution when crossing the sometimes busy road and take in views of the bottomland as it stretches to the Missouri River to the south. At 4.6 miles you'll reach your destination in Matson and retrace your route back to the Weldon Spring trailhead.

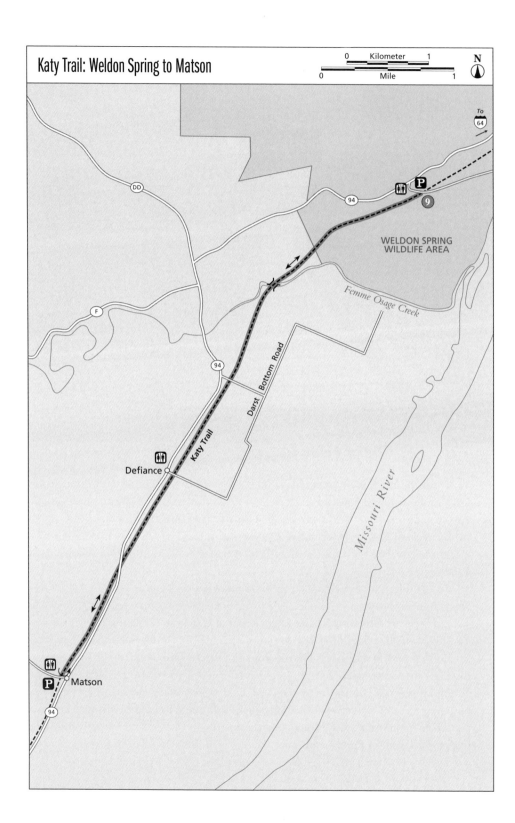

Katy Trail: Weldon Spring to Matson

Miles and Directions

0.0 From the Weldon Spring trailhead, begin hiking west toward the towns of Defiance and Matson.

0.6 Come to the intersection with the Hamburg Trail; continue hiking west.

0.9 Leave the Weldon Spring Wildlife Area.

1.3 Cross Femme Osage Creek and continue hiking west.

2.2 Cross Darst Bottom Road and continue west.

2.9 Come to the town of Defiance.

3.8 Cross MO 94 and continue west.

4.6 Arrive at the Matson trailhead. Return to the Weldon Spring trailhead via the same route.

9.2 Arrive back at the Weldon Spring trailhead.

DANIEL BOONE'S TIES TO MISSOURI

In 1799 Daniel Boone was invited by the Spanish to move to Upper Louisiana, or present-day Missouri. He accepted, and at the age of 65, Daniel Boone; his wife, Rebecca; and several of their children moved from Kentucky to settle near Defiance, Missouri. Today you can learn about Daniel Boone and his family at the Historic Daniel Boone Home and Boonesfield Village (www.lindenwood.edu/boone) in Defiance.

10 Dogwood Trail

One of the more strenuous hikes in Dr. Edmund A. Babler Memorial State Park, the Dogwood Trail offers nature lovers an interesting mix of forest habitat.

Start: Northeast end of parking area
Distance: 2.3-mile lollipop
Hiking time: 1 hour
Difficulty: Moderate due to modest elevation change
Trail surface: Dirt packed trail
Best season: Year-round
Other trail users: Portions of the trail allow equestrians
Canine compatibility: Leashed dogs permitted

Land status: Operated by Missouri State Parks
Fees and permits: None
Maps: USGS Eureka; park map available at visitor center
Trail contact: Dr. Edmund A. Babler Memorial State Park, 800 Guy Park Dr., Wildwood, MO 63005; (636) 458-3813; https://mostateparks.com/park/dr-edmund-babler-memorial-state-park

Finding the trailhead: From St. Louis, take I-64 West / US 40 West for 23 miles to Long Road (exit 16). After 1.4 miles turn right onto Wild Horse Creek Road / Highway CC. Drive 3.1 miles before turning left onto MO 109. Continue for 0.7 mile and then turn right onto Babler Park Drive. After 1.5 miles turn right onto the gated Guy Park Drive and continue straight to the visitor center. From the visitor center, drive 1.5 miles on Guy Park Drive to the large parking area and trailhead. **GPS:** N38 37.369' / W90 41.870'

The Hike

In 1938 Jacob and Henry Babler presented the state of Missouri with 68 acres of hilly countryside as a way to commemorate their brother, Dr. Edmund A. Babler, a well-known and well-loved St. Louis surgeon. Since then the park has grown to 2,500 acres, a precious "green-space oasis" amidst the ever-growing suburbs of St. Louis County. Visiting old-growth forests, which feature white oak, eastern red cedar, sugar maple, walnut, dogwood, pawpaw, and redbud, is a rare treat for park visitors so close to a major urban area. A favorite with birders, Dr. Edmund A. Babler Memorial State Park is home to many species of birds, including downy, red-headed, red-bellied, and pileated woodpeckers.

The Dogwood Trail is one of the best ways to experience the many natural treasures within the park. The 2.3-mile lollipop is the longest and most strenuous hiking trail in the park and provides a good overview of the flora and fauna found in the area. The hike is easily extended by adding the Woodbine Trail to the end of the hike, which shares the same trailhead with the Dogwood Trail.

At the northeast end of the parking area, locate the information kiosk, which marks the trailhead for both the Dogwood Trail (2.3 miles) and the Woodbine Trail (1.8 miles). Marked with green arrows, follow the Dogwood Trail to the north

Emily and Aspen on a Dogwood Trail footbridge

through a typical Missouri hardwood forest. At 0.2 mile come the beginning/end of the loop portion of the Dogwood Trail and turn right (east).

At 0.5 mile the Dogwood Trail merges with an equestrian trail and becomes wider and rockier for 0.2 mile as it ascends the ridge. Near the top of the ridge, pass a stone picnic shelter and restroom. During the 1930s this site was built by groups from the Civilian Conservation Corps, which used the park as a base and constructed many of the roads, trails, and stone structures found here.

HIKING TIP

Gear and clothing are becoming more and more advanced these days. Choose wisely, gear junkies. The light-and-fast gear is pricey but can take less of a toll on your body than out-dated, heavier gear.

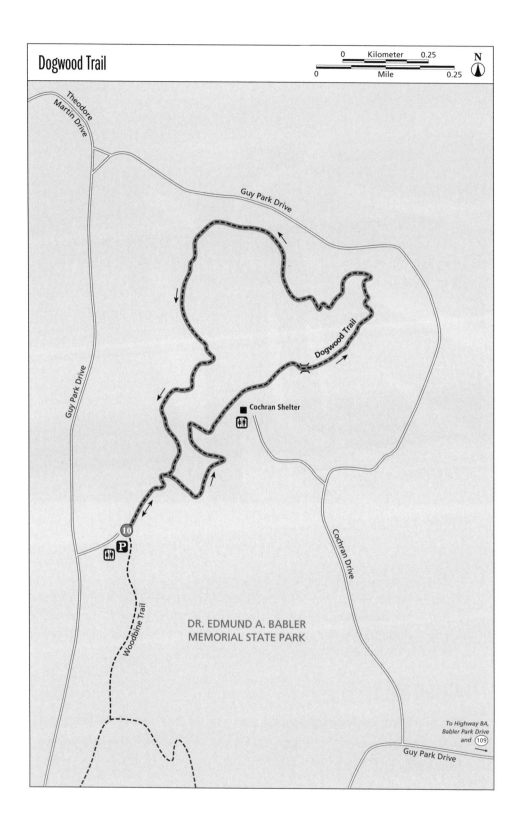

At 1.1 miles come to a spur trail to the right, which leads to the Bates Picnic Area. Stay left (southwest) to continue on the Dogwood Trail. Briefly merge with an equestrian trail at 1.3 miles, then turn right at 1.4 miles to continue on the Dogwood Trail. At 1.5 miles the trail forks again. Turn left (south) to continue.

After hiking 1.6 miles enter a grove of eastern red cedars and cross a small footbridge, which leads you to a fork in the trail. Stay left to continue on the Dogwood Trail. At 2.0 miles reach the end of the Dogwood Trail and return to the parking area. *Option:* If you wish to lengthen your hike, continue on the Woodbine Trail (marked with blue arrows) for an additional 1.8 miles.

Miles and Directions

0.0 From the trailhead, hike north, following the green arrows for the Dogwood Trail.

0.2 Come to the beginning/end of the loop portion of the hike and stay right (east).

0.5 The Dogwood Trail merges briefly with an equestrian trail.

0.7 At the fork in the trail, stay right (northeast) to continue on the Dogwood Trail.

1.1 Avoid the spur trail to the Bates Picnic Area, staying left (southwest) to continue on the Dogwood Trail.

1.3 Merge onto an equestrian trail for 0.1 mile.

1.4 At the fork in the trail, stay right to continue on the Dogwood Trail.

1.5 Turn left (south) to stay on the Dogwood Trail.

1.6 Cross the footbridge and stay left at the fork in the trail to continue on the Dogwood Trail.

2.0 Come to the beginning/end of the loop portion of the hike. Stay right (west) toward the trailhead and parking area. *Option:* To extend your hike by 1.8 miles, continue hiking south on the Woodbine Trail, a loop.

2.3 Arrive back at the trailhead and parking area.

TRAIL ETIQUETTE

When you meet others on the trail, it can sometimes be a tricky social moment. Who has the right-of-way and who should step to the side? On trails that allow multiple users, such as hikers, bikers, and equestrians, the general rule of thumb is that hikers and bikers should yield to horses. Bikers yield to hikers. Following this etiquette can help all users have a safe and enjoyable experience on the trail.

11 Lime Kiln Trail

This fine loop trail offers a peaceful and shaded trek through Rockwoods Reservation, one of the oldest conservation areas in the state of Missouri.

Start: North of trailhead parking area
Distance: 2.8-mile loop
Hiking time: 1.5 hours
Difficulty: Moderate due to modest climb
Trail surface: Dirt packed trail
Best season: Year-round
Other trail users: None
Canine compatibility: Dogs not permitted

Land status: Operated by Missouri Department of Conservation
Fees and permits: None
Maps: USGS Eureka; park map available at visitor center
Trail contact: Rockwoods Reservation, 2751 Glencoe Rd., Wildwood, MO 63038; (636) 458-2236; https://nature.mdc.mo.gov/discover-nature/places/rockwoods-reservation

Finding the trailhead: From St. Louis, take I-44 West for 25 miles to MO 109 (exit 264). Turn right onto MO 109 and drive 4 miles before turning left onto Woods Avenue. Turn right into Rockwoods Reservation on Glencoe Road. Continue 0.5 mile from the park entrance to the trailhead, located on the right. **GPS:** N38 33.482'/W90 39.113'

The Hike

Established in 1938, Rockwoods Reservation consists of 1,880 acres of dense forests, streams, springs, caves, prairie grass, and limestone deposits. Of the several trails in the park, all are worthwhile, but the Lime Kiln Trail offers a more challenging route through some of the best scenery in the area and makes a fantastic day trip just minutes from St. Louis.

The Glencoe Lime and Cement Company was established by the Goetz and Cobb firm in 1880 and was run by Charles W. S. Cobb starting in 1881. The Cobbs came to St. Louis from Maine looking to continue their lucrative lime businesses out west. At the height of its manufacturing, the Glencoe Lime and Cement Company was one of the largest of its type in the state of Missouri. After many successful years the business finally went bankrupt in 1938, and the land on which the facilities were set was some of the first to be designated as property of the Missouri Conservation Commission. Most of the old structures were removed to make way for hiking trails, exhibits, and a new education center. One of the few structures left is the old limekiln found on the Lime Kiln Trail.

Find the trailhead to the north of the small parking area; it is marked with a sign that reads "Lime Kiln Trail 3¼ Miles." Just beyond this sign you will see a large

Limekiln ▶

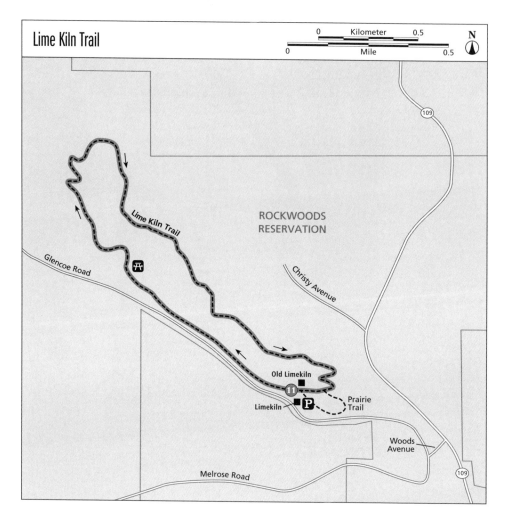

Lime Kiln Trail

0   Kilometer   0.5

0   Mile   0.5

N

ROCKWOODS RESERVATION

Lime Kiln Trail

Glencoe Road

Christy Avenue

Old Limekiln

Limekiln

Prairie Trail

Woods Avenue

Melrose Road

109

109

limekiln, one of the oldest in the area. At the interpretive sign explaining the history of the limekiln, turn left (northwest) and follow the trail as it parallels Glencoe Road. At 0.3 mile rock-hop across a small stream and continue northwest.

GREEN TIP
Q. When you come to a puddle in the middle of the trail, should you walk through it or around it?
A. You should walk through it. Walking around it damages trailside vegetation and can actually cause the puddle to grow wider.

At 1.0 mile cross a drainage and follow the trail as it turns to the northwest and begins a moderately steep ascent up the ridge. At the top of this ridge (1.2 miles), there is a bench that offers a good viewing point in late fall, winter, and early spring. At about 2.5 miles you'll come to a series of switchbacks descending the ridge. Reach the bottom and follow the trail as it curves to the right (west) to return to the trailhead.

Miles and Directions

0.0 From the parking area, follow the trail northwest, passing the old limekiln.

0.3 Cross a shallow stream and continue northwest.

1.0 Cross a drainage and follow the trail as it ascends a moderately steep ridge.

1.2 Reach the bench and viewing area at the top of the ridge.

2.5 Come to the first of a series of switchbacks that descend the ridge.

2.8 Arrive back at the trailhead.

ROCKWOODS RESERVATION TRAILS

Rockwoods Reservation is a fine destination for anyone looking to get out and enjoy the natural beauty of the region. The Lime Kiln Trail is one of our favorites, but there are several other trails worth checking out while you are there. Here is a list of other fine trails you can find in Rockwoods Reservation and their lengths:

Wildlife Habitat Trail, 300 yards

Prairie Trail, 0.25 mile

Rock Quarry Trail (short loop), 1.0 mile

Turkey Ridge Trail, 2.0 miles

Trail Among the Trees, 2.0 miles

Rock Quarry Trail (long loop), 2.25 miles

Green Rock Trail, 3.6 miles in Rockwoods (the trail is 10 miles)

12 Al Foster Trail

Popular with bikers, hikers, runners, and families, the Al Foster Trail provides many options for outdoor recreation. The well-maintained trail follows the Meramec River and offers good views and shade all year long.

Start: Trailhead parking area
Distance: 5.0 miles out and back
Hiking time: 2.5 hours
Difficulty: Easy due to flat terrain
Trail surface: Gravel
Best season: Year-round
Other trail users: Bikers and runners
Canine compatibility: Leashed dogs permitted
Land status: Operated by City of Wildwood, St. Louis County Department of Parks and Recreation, Great Rivers Greenway, and Missouri Department of Natural Resources
Fees and permits: None
Maps: USGS Manchester; maps available at trailhead
Trail contact: City of Wildwood, 16860 Main St., Wildwood, MO 63040; (636) 458-0440; www.cityofwildwood.com/168/Al-Foster-Memorial-Trail

Finding the trailhead: From St. Louis, take I-44 West for about 25 miles to exit 264 toward Eureka. Turn right onto MO 109 and drive 3 miles to Old State Road. Turn right onto Old State Road and then make an immediate right onto Washington Avenue. Washington Avenue becomes Grand Avenue after about 0.2 mile. You'll reach the Al Foster Trail parking area on the left after another 0.2 mile. **GPS:** N38 32.686'/W90 37.525'

The Hike

Managed as a cooperative partnership between the Department of Natural Resources, St. Louis County Parks and Recreation, and the City of Wildwood, the Al Foster Trail provides a fun, flat, and shaded path along the Meramec River. Families with young children will appreciate the wide, flat, crushed-stone trail. Towering limestone bluffs and lush bottomland forests make the Al Foster Trail a nice destination even during the hot and humid summer days that are so common in this part of Missouri.

The future of this relatively new trail looks bright. Connections are planned to Route 66 State Park to the south, and beyond Castlewood State Park to the east. When completed, the Al Foster Trail will become an official segment of the Ozark Trail, which will extend from the confluence of the Meramec and Mississippi Rivers to the Arkansas/Missouri border.

From the trailhead parking area, locate the obvious trail, marked with a large information kiosk. Follow the trail southeast for about 0.1 mile, where it crosses Grand Avenue and passes the Wabash, Frisco, and Pacific Association. This miniature steam locomotive railroad operates every Sunday from May through October and educates visitors about the history of steam locomotives. Continue southeast past the

Wabash, Frisco, and Pacific miniature steam locomotive

Wabash, Frisco, and Pacific Association and follow the crushed limestone trail as it turns to the east and begins to follow the Meramec River.

At 0.4 mile cross the miniature train tracks and continue east, crossing through a meadow. After 1.0 mile come to a fork in the trail. Stay right to continue east on the Al Foster Trail. The trail to the left is the Rock Hollow Trail, which extends about 3 miles to the north.

BREAK TIME!

When hiking, choose a place to take a break with care. In addition to a place in the shade that's free of poison ivy, consider the durability of the ground and the proximity to the trail when taking a break. Avoid vegetation and look for large rock outcroppings, packed dirt, sand, gravel, or other durable surfaces for your break. While the trail is certainly a durable surface, it is more considerate to other hikers to find a place off the trail.

Al Foster Trail

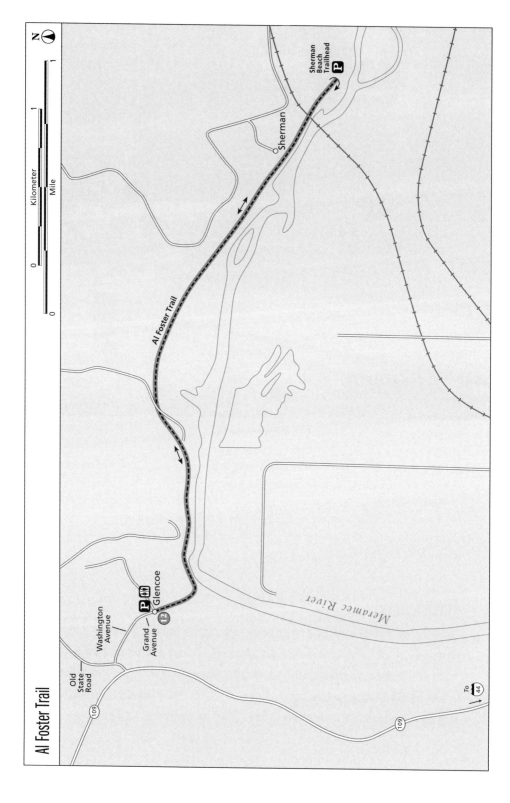

At 1.5 miles cross a small footbridge and continue east for another mile to the Sherman Beach trailhead. From here, turn around and return to the Al Foster trailhead via the same route. If you are looking to extend your hike, you can continue east on the Al Foster Trail through local neighborhoods for an additional 2 miles to Castlewood State Park.

Miles and Directions

0.0 From the trailhead, begin hiking southeast on the obvious gravel trail.

0.1 Cross Grand Avenue and the Wabash, Frisco, and Pacific Railroad.

0.4 Continue east where the trail crosses train tracks.

1.0 Stay right at the fork and continue east on the Al Foster Trail.

1.5 Cross a footbridge and continue east.

2.5 Come to the Sherman Beach trailhead and return via the same route.

5.0 Arrive back at the trailhead parking area.

OZARK TRAIL–PAST, PRESENT, AND FUTURE

The Ozark Trail did not need an act of Congress to get started. Local agencies, landowners, environmental organizations, and volunteers took matters into their own hands and created the Ozark Trail. Construction began in 1981 and currently has nearly 400 miles of completed trail, with several more sections under construction. The long-term vision for the Ozark Trail is to offer a complete trail that runs from St. Louis to the Arkansas border and eventually connects with the Ozark Highland Trail in Arkansas to create a 700-mile through-trail. Much of the trail is open to mountain bikers and equestrian traffic, and all of the trail is open for hiking.

For more information on the Ozark Trail, visit the Ozark Trail Association's website at www.ozarktrail.com.

13 Dogwood Ridge Trail via Losing Stream Trail

The Forest 44 Conservation Area is a rugged forestland located southwest of St. Louis. The 1,008 acres are at the northeastern-most tip of the Ozarks and include many of the plants and animals commonly found in the Ozarks. The area also includes a shooting range and horseback riding.

Start: South end of parking lot
Distance: 2.4-mile lollipop
Hiking time: 1.5 hours
Difficulty: Moderate due to rugged trail
Trail surface: Dirt packed trail and grass
Best season: Spring through fall
Other trail users: None
Canine compatibility: Leashed dogs permitted
Land status: Operated by Missouri Department of Conservation

Fees and permits: None
Maps: USGS Manchester; area map available at trailhead
Trail contact: Missouri Department of Conservation, 2751 Glencoe Rd., Wildwood, MO 63038; (636) 458-2236; http://mdc7.mdc .mo.gov/applications/moatlas/AreaSummary Page.aspx?txtAreaID=9023

Finding the trailhead: From St. Louis, take I-44 West for 17 miles to exit 272. Exit right and then turn left onto MO 141 South. Drive 0.3 mile on MO 141 and turn right onto Meramec Station Road. Drive 1 mile and then turn left onto Hillsboro Road. After 0.4 mile turn right into the Forest 44 Conservation Area parking lot. **GPS:** N38 31.724'/W90 30.787'

The Hike

The Forest 44 Conservation Area is located in west St. Louis County and is just minutes off of I-44. Purchased in 1990, the area was once part of a 10,000-acre cattle ranch. Now, the 1,008-acre area is home to hiking, bird watching, horseback riding, a shooting range, and wildlife viewing.

Numerous springs flow into Williams Creek, which flows along the eastern edge of the conservation area. The creek, forest, hollows, and prairies make for an ideal habitat for many of the animals and birds in the area. Hikers are likely to see songbirds, deer, and wild turkeys during their hike here. Some hikers have claimed that they have spotted minks and herons in the area.

The area is managed by the Missouri Department of Conservation, whose goal is to sustain diverse, healthy plant and animal communities well into the future. The department administers more than 975,000 acres located throughout the state of Missouri, with about 63 percent, or 614,000 acres, of that land being forests.

From the Forest 44 Conservation Area parking lot, locate the Losing Stream Trail at the south end of the lot. The trail is paved and begins heading south. After 0.2 mile

Dogwood Ridge Trail

you'll come to a bridge that crosses over Williams Creek. Look for the spot where you "lose the stream." The stream actually disappears under a rock shelf and reappears downstream. (We'll leave this one for you to discover.)

After 0.3 mile the paved trail ends at a sitting area and connects to the Dogwood Ridge Trail. Turn right onto the Dogwood Ridge Trail here and begin hiking north. At 0.7 mile you will come to a connector trail approaching from the left. Continue hiking southwest and avoid the connector trail. Eventually, at 1.1 miles, the trail turns left (south) and begins ascending Dogwood Ridge. Reach the top and hike along the ridge before beginning the descent at 1.8 miles. At the bottom of the descent, you will also reach the end of the Dogwood Ridge loop at 2.1 miles. Turn right (southeast) back onto the Losing Stream Trail and return to the trailhead at 2.4 miles.

GETTING IN SHAPE

Hiking is the best way to get in shape for hiking, but a good, strong core will take you a long way. Try lunges, sit-ups, and push-ups for starters. We recommend Tina Vindum's exercise guide *Outdoor Fitness* for a well-rounded approach to getting into shape for outdoor adventures.

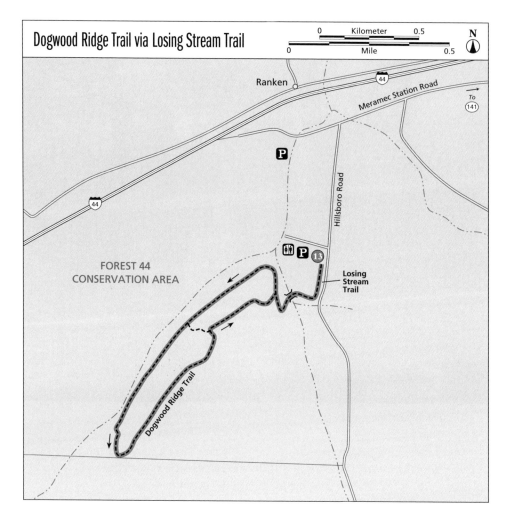

Dogwood Ridge Trail via Losing Stream Trail

Miles and Directions

0.0 From the south end of the parking area, begin hiking south on the paved Losing Stream Trail.

0.2 The trail crosses over a bridge.

0.3 The paved trail ends and connects with the Dogwood Ridge Trail. Turn right (north) onto the Dogwood Ridge Trail.

0.7 Stay right to avoid the short loop connector trail on the left.

1.1 The trail turns left (south) and begins climbing up Dogwood Ridge.

1.8 Begin descent of Dogwood Ridge.

2.1 Reach the end of the Dogwood Ridge loop and turn right (east) back onto the paved Losing Stream Trail.

2.4 Arrive back at the trailhead.

14 Flint Quarry Trail

Passing through the Crescent Hills, the Flint Quarry Trail is an ideal destination for hikers hoping to escape the city and enjoy the natural and cultural history of West Tyson County Park.

Start: Trailhead parking area
Distance: 2.5-mile loop
Hiking time: 2 hours
Difficulty: Moderate due to modest climb
Trail surface: Dirt packed trail
Best season: Fall through spring
Other trail users: Portions of the trail open to mountain bikers and equestrians
Canine compatibility: Leashed dogs permitted

Land status: Operated by St. Louis County Parks
Fees and permits: None
Maps: USGS Manchester; St. Louis County Park maps available online
Trail contact: West Tyson County Park, 131 N. Outer Rd. East, Eureka, MO 63025; (636) 938-5144; www.stlouisco.com/ParksandRecreation/Trails/WestTysonTrails

Finding the trailhead: From St. Louis, take I-44 West to Lewis Road (exit 266). Turn right onto Lewis Road, which quickly becomes West Outer Road, and drive 0.1 mile. The park entrance is on the right. After entering the park, drive 0.1 mile and stay to the right toward the Roth Lodge. Continue 0.2 mile. The road dead-ends at the parking lot and trailhead. Modern restrooms and water are available at the trailhead. **GPS:** N38 30.678' / W90 35.194'

The Hike

The 611-acre West Tyson County Park is a perfect place to visit for hikers looking to escape the crowds found on many of the other, more popular trails in the area. The park tends to be a little overshadowed by the Route 66 State Park, which sits right next door. It also takes on some extra traffic from the popular 7-mile Chubb Trail, which runs through a portion of the park.

Hikers should be on the lookout for wildlife, including white-tailed deer and wild turkeys, as they follow the trail up and around the rocky ridge. A few brief but scenic overlooks can be captured among the forest of oak, hickory, and maple trees.

HIKING TIP

Attention weekend warriors: If you're like us, you have a pretty packed schedule. Between work and family it can be hard to get out on the trails, especially during the week. To minimize the amount of time you spend getting your gear together for a hike, do a gear check after each hike and leave your "go-to" gear packed for the next weekend or spur-of-the-moment hike. Keep your backpack and gear in an easy-to-reach location, so you can just grab it and go!

View from Flint Quarry Trail

Named for the numerous flint quarries found in the area, the Flint Quarry Trail loops through West Tyson County Park. A portion of the park is on the National Register of Historic Places as a result of the hundreds of flint quarries found in the park. Once used by Native Americans, the flint in these hills was mined and shaped into tools and weapons. The flint knapping occurred in the village floodplains and not at the quarry sites, therefore no artifacts occur at the flint mines.

The park is managed by St. Louis County Parks, which administers nearly 13,000 acres of parkland within St. Louis County. More than half of these acres are covered in some form of native vegetation. St. Louis County Parks also runs the 30/30 Hikes Program, which features thirty hikes that take about thirty minutes to complete. This program was designed to fight obesity, and you may see some of the 30/30 Hike signs when you visit St. Louis County parks. You can find maps for many of these hikes on the Parks and Recreation website.

From the parking area, follow the paved trail north to the Flint Quarry Trail. The Flint Quarry Trail branches right (northeast) at 0.1 mile. The obvious dirt-and-rock trail ascends a ridge through maples, chinquapin oaks, and cedars. At 1.4 miles you'll come to the intersection with the Chubb Trail and turn left (southwest) onto that trail. Come to a fork in the trail at 2.2 miles and stay left (south) to continue on the Flint Quarry Trail. At 2.4 miles reach the intersection with the paved walking path and follow it south to return to the trailhead parking area.

Miles and Directions

0.0 From the parking area, begin hiking north on the paved path.

0.1 Turn right (northeast) onto the Flint Quarry Trail, marked with a green quarry symbol.

1.4 Turn left (southwest) onto the Chubb Trail.

2.2 Turn left (south) onto the Flint Quarry Trail.

2.4 Come to the paved walking path. Follow it south.

2.5 Arrive back at the trailhead parking area.

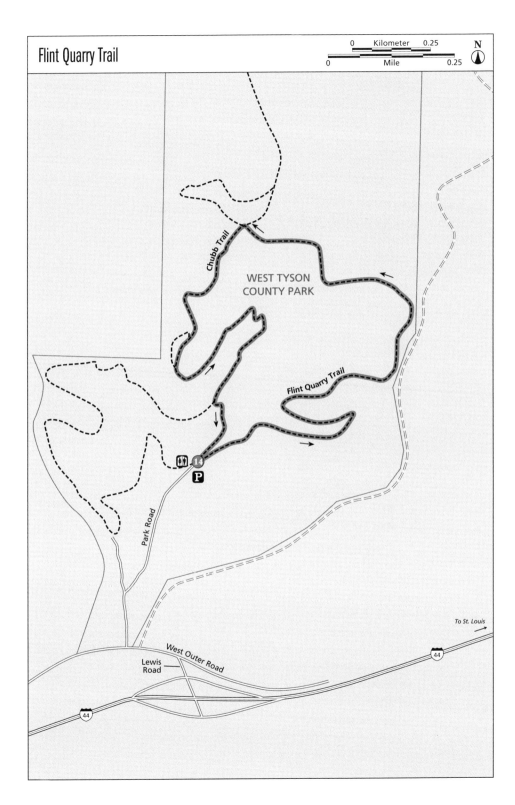

Flint Quarry Trail

0   Kilometer   0.25

0   Mile   0.25

N

Chubb Trail

WEST TYSON
COUNTY PARK

Flint Quarry Trail

14

P

Park Road

To St. Louis

44

West Outer Road

Lewis
Road

44

15 White Bison Trail

Herds of elk and buffalo are undoubtedly an uncommon occurrence in St. Louis County, yet a trip to Lone Elk County Park can offer wildlife lovers sightings of both. The White Bison Trail presents wildlife-viewing opportunities rarely seen in this part of the country.

Start: West side of visitor center parking area
Distance: 3-mile loop
Hiking time: 2 hours
Difficulty: Moderate due to modest climbs
Trail surface: Dirt packed trail
Best season: Year-round
Other trail users: None
Canine compatibility: No dogs permitted in park or on trails

Land status: Operated by St. Louis County Parks
Fees and permits: None
Map: USGS Manchester
Trail contact: Lone Elk County Park, 1 Lone Elk Park Rd., Valley Park, MO 63088; (314) 615-4386; www.stlouisco.com/ParksandRecreation/Trails/LoneElkTrails

Finding the trailhead: From St. Louis, take I-44 West for 17 miles to MO 141 (exit 272). Merge onto North Highway Drive, take a slight right onto MO 141, and then take the ramp to the North Outer Road. Turn left onto Meramec Street and stay straight onto West Outer Road for 2 miles. Turn right onto Lone Elk Park Road. Drive 0.6 mile to the park entrance on the left and drive 0.2 mile more before staying left at the fork. Follow the road for another 0.3 mile, where you will reach the visitor center, parking area, and trailhead. Modern restrooms and water are available at the visitor center. **GPS:** N38 31.873' / W90 32.600'

The Hike

Lone Elk County Park is an interesting park with a peculiar past that offers a memorable day trip for hikers in and around St. Louis. Part of a large cattle operation in the 1800s, the area that now makes up Lone Elk County Park was purchased by the Military Department in 1941 and used as an ammunition depot until the end of World War II. After the war the area was declared a surplus and the park was taken over by St. Louis County Parks.

Taking advantage of the 8-foot-tall perimeter fence, the new park was stocked with ten elk from Yellowstone National Park. In 1951 the park was taken over by the Department of the Army and used once again for military purposes. By the end of the 1950s, the herd had grown to more than one hundred elk and was beginning to run out of food. With winter approaching, it was decided that all the elk would be exterminated and the meat donated to local hospitals. One lone bull escaped this fate and roamed the hills alone for several years.

In 1963 the area was taken over by Washington University, and in 1966 students from the Rockwood School District partnered with the West St. Louis Lions Club to

Bull elk near White Bison Trail

White Bison Trail

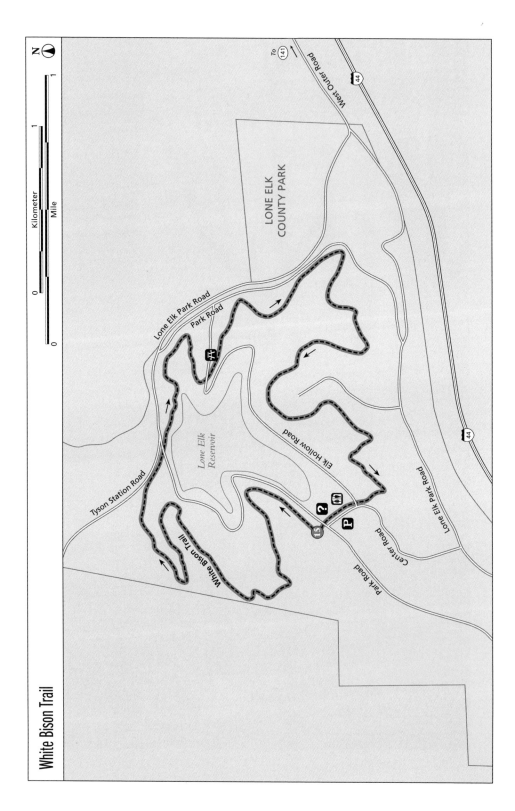

purchase more elk from Yellowstone National Park, bringing the lone elk some much needed company after eight years of solitude.

Today hikers coming to Lone Elk County Park can expect to see elk, white-tailed deer, wild turkeys, waterfowl, and bison. The forest is a typical Missouri hardwood mix, full of oaks and hickories. If visitors want to extend their trip, they can pay a visit to the World Bird Sanctuary to see bald eagles, hawks, owls, and more.

The White Bison Trail loops around Lone Elk Reservoir, and hikers will more than likely pass right by the elk herds that rest near the trail. Visitors will have to enjoy the bison from their vehicles, as the herd is kept separate from the rest of the park.

From the visitor center parking area, locate the White Bison Trail on the west side of Lone Elk Park Road. The trail begins just across a small footbridge, near the picnic area, and is marked with a white buffalo trail marker. It ascends a steep, rocky slope and curves northeast through hickories, oaks, maples, and redbuds, then passes through a woodland area that includes an abundance of pawpaw trees. The trail bends sharply to the right (north) at 0.9 mile and descends the hill.

At 1.1 miles turn right (east) at the park road. Follow the road for 0.1 mile, crossing Lone Elk Park Road and following the trail east into the woods (Lone Elk Reservoir will be to the south of the trail). Cross Elk Hollow Road and a picnic area at 1.6 miles and continue following the trail south. At 2.0 miles the trail turns to the right (west). Come to another park road at 3.0 miles. The visitor center and trailhead parking are just ahead (west).

Miles and Directions

0.0 From the footbridge, begin hiking west.

0.9 The trail bends sharply to the right (north) and descends the hill.

1.1 Come to a park road and turn right (east), following the road up a short hill.

1.2 Cross Lone Elk Park Road and continue east into the woods.

1.6 Cross Elk Hollow Road and a picnic area.

2.0 Follow the trail as it curves to the west.

3.0 Arrive at the visitor center after crossing a park road and continuing west.

A GOOD RULE OF THUMB

Approaching wildlife is never a good idea. A good rule of thumb is that if the wildlife you are viewing changes its behavior in any way, then you are too close or getting too close. A fun way to teach children this rule is by actually using their thumbs. Have your child hold his thumb an arm's distance in front of his face. If he cannot cover up the animal with his thumbnail, he is probably too close and should back up.

It's not an exact science, but it will help kids learn to slow down and think about how close they actually are to potentially dangerous wild animals.

16 River Scene Trail

This loop trail offers visitors a steep climb to scenic limestone bluffs and a flat finish through the floodplain along the Meramec River in Castlewood State Park. Hikers can also take advantage of the numerous picnic areas or take a dip in the Meramec on a hot summer day.

Start: Southwest of trailhead parking area

Distance: 3.4-mile loop

Hiking time: 1.5 hours

Difficulty: Moderate due to modest climb

Trail surface: Dirt packed trail

Best season: Year-round

Other trail users: Portion of the trail allows mountain bikers

Canine compatibility: Leashed dogs permitted

Land status: Operated by Missouri State Parks

Fees and permits: None

Maps: USGS Manchester; park map available at visitor center

Trail contact: Castlewood State Park, 1401 Kiefer Creek Rd., Ballwin, MO 63021; (800) 334-6946; https://mostateparks.com/trails/castlewood-state-park

Finding the trailhead: From St. Louis, take I-44 West for 16.8 miles to exit 272 toward MO 141. Merge onto North Highway Drive and then take a slight right onto MO 141 for 1.8 miles. Take the Big Bend Road ramp, and staying left on West Big Bend Road, drive 2.4 miles to Ries Road. Turn left onto Ries Road for 1 mile, then left onto Kiefer Creek Road into the park. Continue 0.4 mile to the trailhead parking area, picnic shelter, restrooms, and playground on the left (northeast) side of the road. **GPS:** N38 32.993' / W90 32.371'

The Hike

Known as St. Louis's Peaceful Escape, Castlewood State Park is a popular destination for many outdoor enthusiasts in the area. Hikers, equestrians, and bikers share many of the trails in the park. Anglers and paddlers also use the park as an access point for the Meramec River.

The River Scene Trail showcases some of the finest sights in the park. Limestone bluffs, known as the "castles," offer good views of the Meramec River and the Crescent Hills on the other side of the river. The trail gives visitors a taste of the upland forests, consisting of mostly white oak and shagbark hickory trees, as well as a glimpse of bottomland forest, which includes silver maples, box elders, and sycamore trees.

From the trailhead parking area, cross Kiefer Creek Road and locate the signed trailhead for the River Scene Trail to the southwest. Follow the trail to the south as it parallels Kiefer Creek Road, before ascending a moderately steep and rocky ridge. As you near the top of the ridge, the Meramec River comes into view to the south. At 0.3 mile you'll come to the first of several scenic overlooks. At 0.4 mile, where the trail forks, hikers stay left and mountain bikers go right. Come to another fork in the trail at 0.5 mile and stay left. Once again, avoid the bike trail at 0.7 mile and continue

View of the Meramec River from the River Scene Trail

west on the hiking trail. Shortly after this, descend a series of wooden steps and cross a boardwalk at 1.1 miles.

Cross under the railroad tracks at 1.2 miles and follow the trail as it curves to the east. The trail surface at this point alternates between moist sand and dirt, providing excellent opportunities to look for wildlife tracks, such as those of wild turkey, raccoon, and white-tailed deer. After 2.0 miles you'll come to an intersection with a connector trail. Stay right and follow the red arrows to continue on the River Scene Trail.

GREEN TIP
Missouri state parks alone receive almost 16 million
annual visits from public users. That's 16 million reasons why
hikers should practice a minimal impact ethic like
Leave No Trace. The Leave No Trace Center for Outdoor Ethics has
lots of information on how you can minimize your
impact while enjoying the outdoors. To learn more,
visit their website at lnt.org.

River Scene Trail

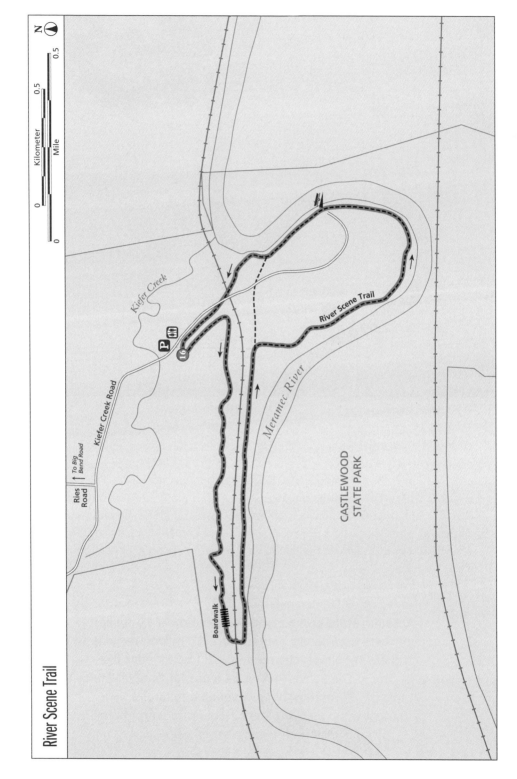

Kiefer Creek

Ries Road

To Big Bend Road

Kiefer Creek Road

P 16

Boardwalk

Meramec River

River Scene Trail

CASTLEWOOD STATE PARK

N

Kilometer
0   0.5

Mile
0   0.5

Come to a river access point at 2.8 miles and continue north, passing an information kiosk. At 3.2 miles the trail comes to Kiefer Road and crosses under the railroad tracks. Cross Kiefer Road on the north side of the railroad tracks and follow the trail back to the trailhead parking area.

Miles and Directions

0.0 From the signed trailhead, turn left and follow the River Scene Trail south.

0.3 Come to the first of several scenic overlooks.

0.4 Come to a fork in the trail, where hikers stay left.

0.5 Come to another fork in the trail; hikers stay left.

0.7 Avoid the bike trail to the right (north) and continue west on the hiking trail.

1.1 Come to a boardwalk.

1.2 Cross under the railroad tracks and follow the trail as it curves to the east.

2.0 At the intersection with a connector trail, stay right (south), following the red arrows.

2.8 Come to the river access point and continue north on a paved trail.

3.0 At the fork in the trail, stay right (north) on the dirt trail.

3.2 Come to Kiefer Road, cross under the railroad tracks, and then cross the road. The trail continues to the northwest.

3.4 Arrive back at the trailhead.

CASTLEWOOD STATE PARK TRAILS

Castlewood State Park is becoming a hot spot for outdoor recreation in the St. Louis area. The 1,880-acre park currently offers nearly 30 miles of trails. The trails here vary from flat and easy to steep and technical. While many of the trails are a popular destination for mountain bikers, hikers will find that most of the trails can accommodate both hikers and bikers. The River Scene Trail is one of our favorites, but there are many other trails worth checking out in the park. Here is a list of other fine trails you can find in Castlewood State Park:

Lone Wolf Trail, 1.5 miles

Cedar Bluff Loop, 2.25 miles

Stinging Nettle Trail, 2.5 miles

Castlewood Loop, 2.75 miles

Gropeter Trail, 3.75 miles

Al Foster Trail, 4.5 miles

Chubb Trail, 7.0 miles

17 Hickory Ridge Trail

The Powder Valley Conservation Area considers itself an urban oasis. Open since 1991, the area offers 112 acres of oak-hickory forest to hikers. The Powder Valley Conservation Nature Center offers numerous educational opportunities for visitors to enhance their knowledge about the use of resources in an urban setting.

Start: Southern end of parking area
Distance: 1.2-mile lollipop
Hiking time: 1 hour
Difficulty: Moderate due to modest climb
Trail surface: Paved
Best season: Year-round
Other trail users: None
Canine compatibility: No pets allowed
Land status: Operated by Missouri Department of Conservation

Fees and permits: None
Maps: USGS Kirkwood; trail map available at nature center
Trail contact: Powder Valley Conservation Nature Center, Missouri Department of Conservation, 11715 Cragwold Rd., Kirkwood, MO 63122-7015; (314) 301-1500; https://nature.mdc.mo.gov/discover-nature/places/powder-valley-cnc

Finding the trailhead: From St. Louis, take I-44 West for 12 miles to exit 277B. Turn left onto South Lindbergh Boulevard. Drive 0.2 mile and turn right onto Watson Road. After 0.4 mile turn right onto South Geyer Road. Go 0.2 mile and then turn left onto Cragwold Road. Drive for 0.8 mile and turn right into the Powder Valley Conservation Area on Cragwold Road. Arrive at the Powder Valley Conservation Nature Center after 0.2 mile. **GPS:** N38 33.337'/W90 25.701'

The Hike

The Powder Valley Conservation Nature Center is a hidden gem in St. Louis. Located right off of I-44 and I-270, there are not even any signs along the roadways to advertise the area. Run by the Missouri Department of Conservation, since 1991 the nature center has educated more than one million visitors on the wise use of our urban resources.

All of the trails are paved, offering easy access for strollers and wheelchairs (the Hickory Ridge Trail has a steep incline and decline though). There are also plenty of benches along the trails to encourage visitors to take their time and soak in the outdoors. The nature center, interpretive displays, and oak-hickory forest make for the perfect brief getaway.

After visiting the nature center, make your way to the southern end of the parking area and locate the Hickory Ridge trailhead. Begin hiking south on the trail and immediately cross a bridge that goes over Cragwold Road. Continue east and reach the loop portion of the trail at 0.1 mile. Arrows direct hiking traffic to the right (south). Hike south and reach an intersection at 0.3 mile. Turning left will take you on a short loop back to the trailhead, so stay straight (southeast) on the longer loop.

Hickory Ridge Trail

The trail descends Hickory Ridge, and at 0.5 mile you will reach the first of a series of bridges that cross back and forth over a small stream. Continue hiking through the hollow as it ascends back up Hickory Ridge, reaching the end of the longer loop at 1.0 mile. Turn right (northwest; left will return you to the longer loop again) and follow the trail back to the parking area at 1.2 miles.

GREEN TIP

It is so cute to see a little squirrel nibbling away on the food that other hikers/campers left behind, but did you know about the damage that is caused by doing so? Not only do animals that become habituated to human food become a campground nuisance, but our food is not natural to their environment and is therefore not good for them. Keep humans and animals safe by never feeding wildlife and storing your food in an area where wildlife cannot reach it.

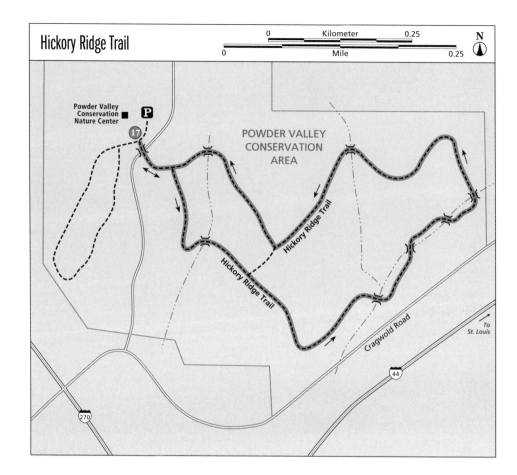

Miles and Directions

0.0 From the south end of the parking area, begin hiking southeast on the Hickory Ridge Trail.

0.1 Reach the loop portion of the trail and stay right (south).

0.3 Stay right (southeast) on the longer Hickory Ridge loop.

0.5 Cross the first of a series of bridges.

1.0 Reach the end of the long loop and stay right (northwest) to return to the trailhead.

1.2 Arrive back at the trailhead parking area.

TEN BIRDS TO LOOK FOR AT POWDER VALLEY CONSERVATION NATURE CENTER

The Powder Valley Conservation Nature Center provides important habitat for birds in the St. Louis area. Here are ten birds to keep an eye out for while hiking:

1. Wild turkey
2. Blue jay
3. Great-tailed grackle
4. Northern cardinal
5. Red-bellied woodpecker
6. Downy woodpecker
7. Hairy woodpecker
8. Pileated woodpecker
9. Red-tailed hawk
10. Ruby-throated hummingbird

18 Spring Valley Trail

Managed by St. Louis County Parks, Cliff Cave County Park is home to the second-largest cave in St. Louis County. Although the cave itself is closed to protect the endangered Indiana bat, this short loop makes a fine day trip and is only minutes from the city.

Start: West from trailhead parking area
Distance: 2.1-mile lollipop
Hiking time: 1.5 hours
Difficulty: Moderate due to modest climb
Trail surface: Dirt packed trail
Best season: Fall through spring
Other trail users: Mountain bikers and equestrians
Canine compatibility: Leashed dogs permitted

Land status: Operated by St. Louis County Parks
Fees and permits: None
Maps: USGS Oakville; St. Louis County park maps available online
Trail contact: Cliff Cave County Park, 806 Cliff Cave Rd., St. Louis, MO 63129; (314) 846-8337; www.stlouisco.com/ParksandRecreation/Trails/CliffCaveTrails

Finding the trailhead: From St. Louis, take I-55 South for 10 miles to exit 197 toward I-255 East. Take I-255 East for 2.7 miles to the Telegraph Road exit. Drive 1.9 miles south on Telegraph Road to Cliff Cave Road and turn left. Follow Cliff Cave Road for 1.1 miles to the park gate and another 0.4 mile to the trailhead and parking on the right. **GPS:** N38 27.546'/W90 17.461'

The Hike

Cliff Cave County Park received the "Best View of the Mississippi" award in 2009 for good reason: The Mississippi River provides the entire eastern border of the park. The 525-acre park opened to the public in 1977 after being bought for $400,000 in 1972. The cave was used as a riverside tavern by French traders in the 1700s and as a wine cellar in the 1800s, and is a habitat for the endangered Indiana bat today.

Hikers enjoy the shade of oaks, hickories, and dogwoods in the forested portions of the park. Visitors that choose to hike along the Mississippi River Trail will encounter beautifully restored wetland prairies that were once very common in these floodplains. The cave itself is closed to visitors, both to protect the rare bat population inside and to protect the cave itself from vandalism. But if you visit in the winter, you can witness the cave "breathing" a cold mist.

The Spring Valley Trail is a 2.1-mile lollipop hike. This trail features Indian Cave, also known as Cliff Cave, which hikers can look into at either the start or the end of the hike, as the loop begins and ends here. The trail is the most strenuous hike in the park and the most urban, as you will pass several social trail intersections that lead to nearby neighborhoods and are used by locals to access the trail.

Redbud tree

The park is managed by St. Louis County Parks, which administers nearly 13,000 acres of parkland within St. Louis County. More than half of these acres are covered in some form of native vegetation. St. Louis County Parks also runs the 30/30 Hikes

Cliff Cave

Program, which features thirty hikes that take about thirty minutes to complete. This program was designed to fight obesity, and you may see some of the 30/30 Hike signs when you visit St. Louis County parks. You can find maps for many of these hikes on the Parks and Recreation website.

From the trailhead parking area, locate the Spring Valley Trail sign and follow the arrow west as you walk along Cliff Cave Road. Just before the guardrails, the trail turns to the left and is marked with an orange diamond and a blue square. At 0.1 mile cross a shallow creek and follow the trail to the right (north) as it ascends the ridge. Be careful to avoid several unmarked spur trails in this area. At 0.2 mile reach the actual beginning of the loop and stay to the right. You will notice dogwoods, shagbark hickories, and sassafras as you meander through the karst topography of the area.

The trail passes behind several houses as it skirts the edge of a suburb and briefly reminds you that you are in fact only minutes from the city. At 1.7 miles reach a sign that reads "Park Exit, Susan Road Access," turn left (north), and stay on the Spring

223 BILLION REASONS TO LOVE BATS
According to the Missouri Department of Conservation, Missouri's 775,000 gray bats eat more than 223 billion bugs (540 tons) each year.

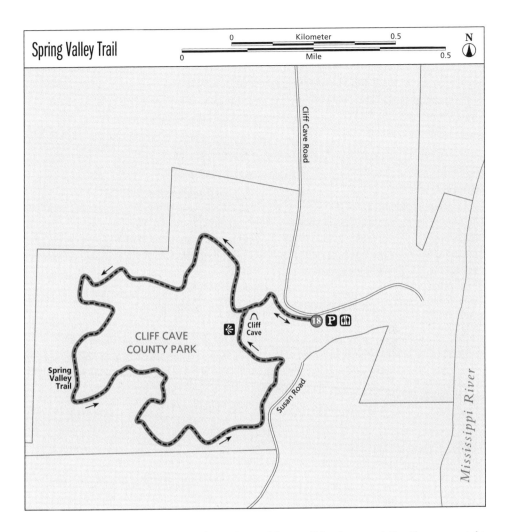

Spring Valley Trail

Valley Trail. Reach a sign marking the end/start of the loop at 1.9 miles, turn right (east), and follow the trail back to Cliff Cave Road and the trailhead parking area.

Miles and Directions

0.0   From the parking area, follow Cliff Cave Road west and turn left onto the Spring Valley Trail.

0.1   Cross a creek and follow the trail north, ascending a ridge.

0.2   At the beginning of the loop portion of the hike, stay right (north).

1.7   Avoid the spur trail signed "Park Exit, Susan Road Access," turning left (north) to stay on the Spring Valley Trail.

1.9   Reach the end of the loop portion of the hike and turn right (east) to return to the trailhead and parking area.

2.1   Arrive back at the trailhead and parking area.

19 Limestone Hill Trail

Mastodon State Historic Site is located just off of I-55 and is a short drive from downtown St. Louis. The longest trail in Mastodon State Historic Site, the Limestone Hill Trail offers a rugged but scenic hike that traverses the base of an interesting limestone bluff.

Start: North end of parking area
Distance: 2-mile loop
Hiking time: 1.5 hours
Difficulty: Difficult due to modest climb and rugged terrain
Trail surface: Dirt packed trail
Best season: Fall through spring
Other trail users: None
Canine compatibility: Leashed dogs permitted

Land status: Operated by Missouri State Parks
Fees and permits: None
Maps: USGS Lake Killarney; trail map available at visitor center
Trail contact: Mastodon State Historic Site, 1050 Museum Dr., Imperial, MO 63052; (636) 464-2976; https://mostateparks.com/trails/mastodon-state-historic-site?type=hiking

Finding the trailhead: From St. Louis, take I-55 South for 20.7 miles to Imperial Main Street at exit 186. Turn right onto Imperial Main Street and then take an immediate right onto West Outer Road. Drive 0.6 mile on West Outer Road to a stop sign and turn left onto Seckman Road. Follow Seckman Road for 0.8 mile into the park and to the parking area on the left. **GPS:** N38 22.821' / W90 23.690'

The Hike

In the early 1800s the bones of ancient mastodons were found just south of St. Louis at what is now Mastodon State Historic Site. The mastodons were large, tusked mammals, similar in size and appearance to the mammoth and the elephant. The Kimmswick Bone Bed, located at the site, is a Pleistocene Ice Age deposit.

The site quickly gained fame among scientists from around the world in 1979 when a 10,000- to 14,000-year-old stone spear point was excavated. This stone point confirmed the existence of humans, known as the Clovis people, and mastodons during the same time period. These findings suggested that the Clovis people hunted these massive animals and that this may have played a role in these animals becoming extinct near the end of the Ice Age.

The museum at Mastodon State Historic Site is the only museum in Missouri dedicated to the last Ice Age and is an excellent resource for learning more about this unique area.

The 431-acre Mastodon State Historic Site offers three hiking trails. Hikes range from short and simple strolls along the bone beds and the Callison Memorial Bird

JD on the Limestone Hill Trail ▶

Limestone Hill Trail

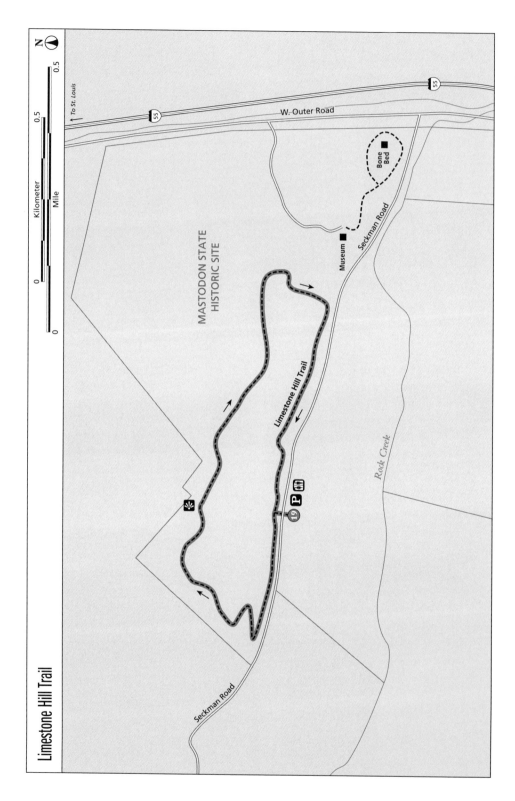

Sanctuary to the longer Limestone Hill Trail. Hikers can expect the usual mixed hardwood forests of oak, hickory, and maple trees. For a small entry fee, visitors can stop by the museum to view mastodon fossils, bones, and other artifacts.

The Limestone Hill Trail is a 2-mile loop hike that begins at the only picnic site in the small park. This is the longest and most strenuous hike in the park. The Limestone Hill Trail and Spring Branch Trail share the same trailhead and can easily be combined to extend your hike by 0.75 mile.

From the north end of the parking area, locate the information kiosk and trailhead marker. Follow the obvious gravel trail and the trail markers for the Limestone Hill Trail west and then north to cross Seckman Road (0.1 mile). On the other side of Seckman Road, turn left (west) and follow the trail as it parallels the road. At 0.3 mile the trail curves to the right (north) and ascends the hill to a bench and scenic overlook at 0.7 mile. Stay right to avoid this spur trail and continue southeast on the Limestone Hill Trail. At 1.2 miles at another fork in the trail, stay right and follow the trail marker, which points south, down a gradual hill. At 1.9 miles return to Seckman Road, cross the road, and continue south to the trailhead parking area.

Miles and Directions

0.0 From the trailhead, begin hiking west, then north toward Seckman Road.

0.1 Cross Seckman Road and turn left (west).

0.3 Follow the trail as it curves to the right (north) and ascends a hill.

0.7 Come to a bench and scenic overlook.

1.2 At the fork in the trail, stay right to continue on Limestone Hill Trail.

1.9 Cross Seckman Road and continue south.

2.0 Arrive back at the trailhead.

20 Wilderness Trail

The Wilderness Trail in Meramec State Park is a beautiful 8.6-mile hike through a portion of the park's 6,896 acres. While the park offers several miles of hiking/backpacking trails and numerous backcountry camping sites, the caves tend to be the biggest draw to the park. More than forty caves, including the popular Fisher Cave, grace the area.

Start: North from trailhead parking area
Distance: 8.6-mile lollipop
Hiking time: 5 hours
Difficulty: More challenging due to length
Trail surface: Dirt packed trail
Best season: Spring through fall
Other trail users: None
Canine compatibility: Leashed dogs permitted

Land status: Operated by Missouri State Parks
Fees and permits: None
Maps: USGS Meramec State Park; trail map available at park office
Trail contact: Meramec State Park, 115 Meramec Park Dr., Sullivan, MO 63080; (573) 468-6072; https://mostateparks.com/trails/meramec-state-park?type=backpacking

Finding the trailhead: From St. Louis, take I-44 West for 64 miles to exit 226 toward Sullivan. Turn left onto MO 185 South and drive 3.3 miles to the park entrance on the right. Follow Meramec Drive for 0.3 mile and turn left at the stop sign. After 1 mile turn left into the parking area for the Wilderness Trail. **GPS:** N38 12.766' / W91 5.609'

The Hike

Located on the northern perimeter of the Ozarks, the 6,896-acre Meramec State Park is one of Missouri's natural treasures. Flanked on the east side by the Meramec River, this area is known for rich glades, mature hardwood forests, and numerous caves. Wildlife is abundant in the park, and you may encounter a bobcat, white-tailed deer, or even a black bear as you explore this area. Some of the caves are open for exploration, and you may encounter rare species of bats there.

The Wilderness Trail is the longest trail in the park and the only one designated for backpacking. Eight backpacking campsites are provided along the trail, although it is possible to hike it in a single day if you're looking for a more challenging day hike. If you chose to hike on the Wilderness Trail, you will not be disappointed, as the trail cuts through the most rugged and remote areas of the park. From the Meramec Upland Forest Natural Area to Copper Hollow and Copper Hollow Spring, there are new sights at every bend in the trail.

From the Wilderness Trail parking area and trailhead, begin hiking north on the Wilderness Trail. At 0.2 mile you will reach the trail register, where you should sign

Missouri's bright foliage ▶

Glade crossing on the Wilderness Trail

in, and continue hiking west. You will reach the loop portion of the trail at 0.4 mile. Bear left (northwest) and make your way past the first two backcountry campsites at 0.6 and 0.7 mile. Pass the trail access to the campsites and make your way into and out of Campbell Hollow before reaching and crossing MO Spur Route 185 at 2.0 miles.

Continue hiking north and pass by a white-blazed connector trail on the right at 2.4 miles before you reach a series of backcountry campsites at miles 2.5, 3.3, 3.4, and 3.7. After the last backcountry campsite, the trail will begin a steep descent down into Copper Hollow. As the hollow opens up at 4.3 miles, you'll come to Copper Hollow Spring. From the spring, continue hiking east to catch a quick glimpse of the Meramec River before the trail turns west.

At 6.2 miles you will reach the white-blazed connector trail again and then cross MO Spur Route 185 again at 6.8 miles. Hike southeast after crossing the road toward the last backcountry campsite at 7.4 miles and then cross Ridge Road (a service road) at 7.7 miles. The trail continues south and then southeast to the end of the loop at 8.2 miles. Return to the trailhead and parking area at 8.6 miles.

GREEN TIP
Did you know that a plastic water bottle can take up to
500 years to decompose?
Solution: Invest in a refillable water bottle and faucet filter. Save a
ton of money and the environment at the same time.

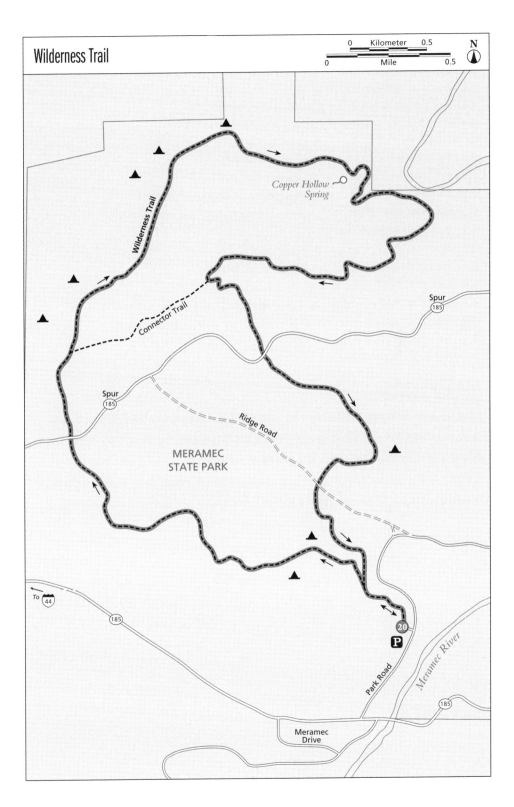

Wilderness Trail

0 Kilometer 0.5

0 Mile 0.5

N

Copper Hollow Spring

Wilderness Trail

Connector Trail

Spur 185

Spur 185

Ridge Road

MERAMEC STATE PARK

To 44

185

20

P

Park Road

Meramec River

185

Meramec Drive

Miles and Directions

0.0 From the Wilderness Trail parking area and trailhead, begin hiking north.

0.2 Reach the trail register and sign in.

0.4 Stay left (northwest) where the loop portion of the trail begins.

0.6 The trail to the right leads to a backcountry campsite; there's another one at 0.7 mile, to the left.

2.0 The trail crosses MO Spur Route 185. Continue north.

2.4 A connector trail enters from the right.

2.5 The trails to the left (west) go to backcountry campsites.

3.3 The trails to the left lead to backcountry campsites at 3.3, 3.4, and 3.7 miles.

4.3 Reach Copper Hollow Spring.

6.2 A connector trail comes in from the right (west).

6.8 The trail crosses MO Spur Route 185. Continue southeast.

7.4 The trail to the left (east) leads to the last backcountry campsite.

7.7 The trail crosses over Ridge Road. Continue south.

8.2 Reach the end of the loop. Turn left (southeast) back toward the trailhead.

8.6 Arrive back at the trailhead and parking area.

NEARBY TRAILS

All of the trails in Meramec State Park are designated for hiking use only. In addition to the Wilderness Trail, the park offers several other trails that are worthy of mention. The Bluff Trail is a 1.5-mile loop trail that offers several scenic overlooks; the 1.8-mile Deer Hollow Trail serves as a connector trail between the dining lodge and Fisher Cave; and the Natural Wonders Trail is a 1.3-mile loop trail that feature caves, glades, and mature hardwood forests.

21 Rockywood Trail

Widely regarded as Missouri's petroglyph showcase due to the largest known collection of carvings in the state, Washington State Park tends to be a memorable visit for many visitors. In addition to the 1,000-year-old petroglyphs, the park also offers rugged Ozark terrain to hiking enthusiasts. The Rockywood Trail is the longest trail in the park.

Start: Northwest from Thunderbird Lodge parking area
Distance: 6.3-mile loop
Hiking time: 3.5 hours
Difficulty: Difficult due to the length of the trail
Trail surface: Dirt packed trail and road crossings
Best season: Year-round
Other trail users: None
Canine compatibility: Leashed dogs permitted
Land status: Operated by Missouri State Parks
Fees and permits: None
Maps: USGS Tiff; trail map available at Thunderbird Lodge
Trail contact: Washington State Park, 13041 State Highway 104, DeSoto, MO 63020; (636) 586-2995; https://mostateparks.com/trails/washington-state-park?type=hiking

Finding the trailhead: From St. Louis, take I-55 South for about 33 miles to exit 174B toward US 67 South. Follow US 67 South for 6.1 miles and turn right onto MO 110. Follow MO 110 for 6.3 miles and turn left onto MO 21. After 10.5 miles turn right onto MO 104 into Washington State Park. Continue 1.1 miles to the Thunderbird Lodge parking area and Rockywood trailhead.
GPS: N38 5.126' / W90 41.061'

The Hike

Located near De Soto, Missouri, Washington State Park has a rich cultural and natural history. Several Native American rock carvings, or petroglyphs, have been found in the park, and unlike many of the rock carvings found in this part of the country, they have largely escaped vandalism. The petroglyphs are thought to have been made by the Middle Mississippi culture around AD 1000.

The Rockywood Trail is the longest and most rugged trail in the park and is designed for both hiking and backpacking. Highlights of the trail include beautiful

WHAT'S THE DIFFERENCE BETWEEN A PETROGLYPH AND A PICTOGRAPH?

Both terms refer to rock art produced by Native Americans in the past. Petroglyphs are pictures or symbols that have been carved into the rock. Pictographs are painted onto the rock surface.

Rough green snake on the Rockywood Trail

open glades, rugged hardwood woodlands, and several scenic overlooks. A short detour from the trail will take you to one of the park's most popular interpretive areas, which contains over a dozen petroglyphs carved into slabs of limestone.

From the Thunderbird Lodge parking lot, locate the trailhead on the west side of the lodge. Begin hiking northwest behind the Thunderbird Lodge to a set of stairs leading up the bluff. The trail crosses Dugout Road at 0.5 mile and then reaches a trail junction at 0.8 mile. Continue hiking west; the trail to the left (south) is the Opossum Trail. At 2.2 miles the trail makes a sharp left and continues south.

CIVILIAN CONSERVATION CORPS

As part of President Franklin D. Roosevelt's New Deal, the Civilian Conservation Corps (CCC) was created in the 1930s to combat the problem of unemployed males between the ages of 18 and 25. The CCC did various public works projects across the country, and much of their work can be seen in Missouri's state parks today.

An African-American company of the Civilian Conservation Corps was responsible for the development of Washington State Park. Not long after the land was designated a state park in 1932, the CCC crew started working and used the petroglyphs in the park as their inspiration. The crew named their barracks Camp Thunderbird, and that theme still exists today at places like the Thunderbird Lodge.

Rockywood Trail

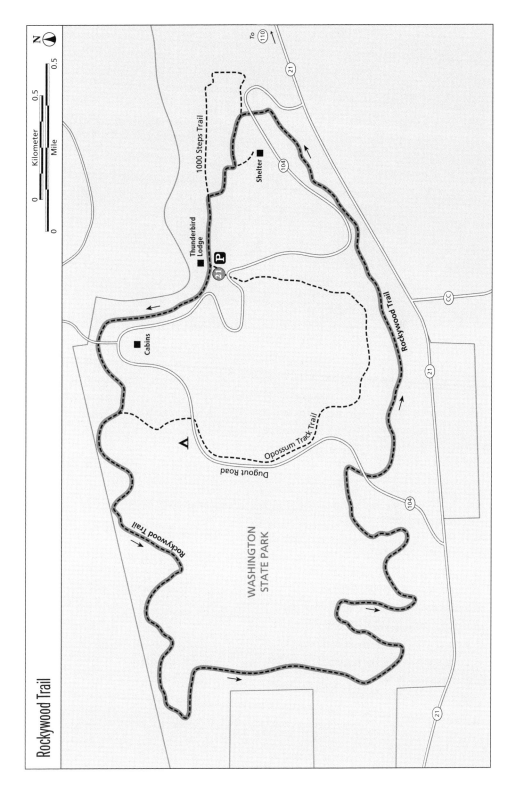

Thistle

Hiking east along the trail, you cross MO 104 at 4.3 miles and then again at 5.7 miles. The Rockywood Trail joins the 1000 Steps Trail at 5.8 miles, where you turn left (west) to continue down the 1000 Steps. When you reach the bottom of the steps, turn left (west) at 6.1 miles and continue on to the east side of the parking area and the end of the Rockywood Trail at 6.3 miles.

Miles and Directions

0.0 From the Thunderbird Lodge parking area and trailhead, begin hiking northwest on the Rockywood Trail.

0.5 Cross Dugout Road and continue hiking west.

0.8 Continue straight (west) on the Rockywood Trail. The Opossum Trail splits to the left (south).

2.2 The trail turns to the left (south).

4.3 The trail crosses MO 104. Continue south.

5.7 The trail crosses MO 104 again. Continue north.

5.8 Turn left (west) and descend the 1000 Steps Trail.

6.1 Turn left (west) at the bottom of the 1000 Steps.

6.3 Arrive back at the parking area.

22 1000 Steps Trail

The 1000 Steps Trail, in historic Washington State Park, climbs one of the towering dolomite bluffs located in the park. The strenuous trek takes hikers to the top of the bluff to a lookout area with views of the Big River and camping area. The trail continues on to pass some of the structures built by an African-American company of the Civilian Conservation Corps in the 1930s.

Start: Northeast end of Thunderbird Lodge parking area
Distance: 1.4-mile lollipop
Hiking time: 1 hour
Difficulty: Difficult due to steep climb
Trail surface: Dirt packed trail and rock
Best season: Year-round
Other trail users: None
Canine compatibility: Leashed dogs permitted

Land status: Operated by Missouri State Parks
Fees and permits: None
Maps: USGS Tiff; trail map available at Thunderbird Lodge
Trail contact: Washington State Park, 13041 State Highway 104, DeSoto, MO 63020; (636) 586-2995; https://mostateparks.com/trails/washington-state-park?type=hiking

Finding the trailhead: From St. Louis, take I-55 South for about 33 miles to exit 174B toward US 67 South. Follow US 67 South for 6.1 miles and turn right onto MO 110. Follow MO 110 for 6.3 miles and turn left onto MO 21. After 10.5 miles turn right onto MO 104 into Washington State Park. Continue 1.1 miles to the Thunderbird Lodge parking area and 1000 Steps trailhead. **GPS:** N38 5.127' / W90 41.046'

The Hike

Located in the eastern Ozarks, the 1,875-acre Washington State Park is rich in both natural and cultural history. Several Native American rock carvings, or petroglyphs, have been found within the park, and unlike many of the rock carvings found in this part of the country, they have largely escaped vandalism. Visitors hoping to see these artifacts can locate them just behind the visitor center or at the park's main interpretive site, which is accessible both by vehicle and foot. These petroglyphs, the largest grouping found in Missouri to date, were created by the Middle Mississippi culture around AD 1000 and give clues to the beliefs and lives of the people living here during that time. Due to the number and exceptional quality of the carvings, these sites have been placed on the National Register of Historic Places and are protected under the National Historic Preservation Act.

In more recent history the park benefited from the work of African-American Civilian Conservation Corps stonemasons. In the 1930s the Civilian Conservation Corps built the Thunderbird Lodge, several stone hiking shelters, and a stone picnic pavilion, along with several other structures in the park. They also laid the impressive

Thunderbird petroglyph in Washington State Park

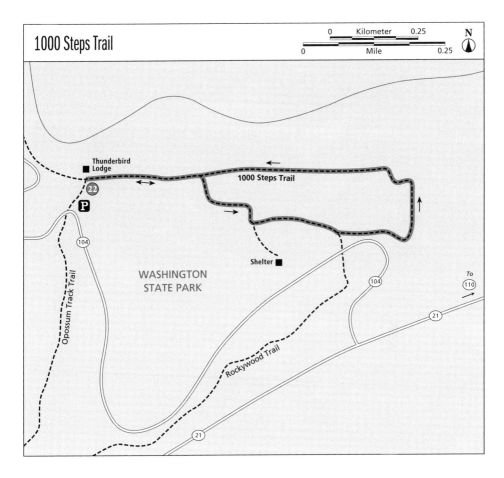

stone slabs that make up the steps on the 1000 Steps Trail. In honor of the beauty and outstanding quality of the craftsmanship, these stone structures were placed on the National Register of Historic Places in 1985.

Locate the 1000 Steps Trail at the northeast end of the Thunderbird Lodge parking area. Follow the trail east, along the edge of a floodplain of the Big River. At 0.2 mile reach the loop portion of the trail and turn right (south) to begin the ascent of the 1000 Steps. After 0.5 mile reach the top of the stairs and bear left (east) to stay on the 1000 Steps Trail and avoid the Rockywood Trail on the right.

Continue past some of the old African-American Civilian Conservation Corps buildings as you approach a trail to the park office on the right. Turn left (north) here, at 0.6 mile, to descend back down to the floodplain. When you reach the bottom, keep hiking west through the Washington hardwoods, with views of the campground to the north. Reach the end of the loop at 1.2 miles and return to the trailhead at 1.4 miles.

Miles and Directions

0.0 From the north end of the Thunderbird Lodge parking area, begin hiking east on the 1000 Steps Trail.

0.2 Reach the loop portion of the trail and turn right (south) up the 1000 Steps.

0.5 Stay left (east) on the 1000 Steps Trail; the Rockywood Trail is to the right.

0.6 Turn left (north); turning right leads to the park office.

1.2 Reach the end of the loop.

1.4 Arrive back at the trailhead.

GREEN TIP

Don't move firewood! The emerald ash borer is an invasive insect that is responsible for killing millions of ash trees in the United States over the last decade. It can be transported to new areas by hitching a ride in firewood. In order to stop the spread of the emerald ash borer, only use firewood from local forests—firewood that has been cut within a 50-mile radius of the place you plan to have a campfire. In addition, if you have any firewood left over after a camping trip and you do not live in the area, do not bring the firewood home with you, as you could risk infecting ash trees in your area.

◄ *Groundhog taking cover in a tree on the 1000 Steps Trail*

23 Mooner's Hollow Trail

Once a popular spot for moonshine production, this loop trail follows the cold, clear waters of Coonville Creek through a lovely mixed hardwood forest.

Start: Northeast from trailhead parking area
Distance: 3-mile loop
Hiking time: 1.5 hours
Difficulty: Moderate due to modest climbs
Trail surface: Dirt packed trail
Best season: Fall through spring
Other trail users: None
Canine compatibility: Leashed dogs permitted

Land status: Operated by Missouri State Parks
Fees and permits: None
Map: USGS Bonne Terre
Trail contact: St. Francois State Park, 8920 US 67 North, Bonne Terre, MO 63628; (573) 358-2173; https://mostateparks.com/trails/st-francois-state-park

Finding the trailhead: From St. Louis, take I-55 South for 33 miles to US 67 South, exit 174B. Drive on US 67 South for 19.3 miles before turning left onto Park Road. Drive 0.4 mile on Park Road to the parking area and trailhead on the left. **GPS: N37 58.212'/W90 31.992'**

The Hike

The first acres of St. Francois State Park were purchased in 1964 in a community effort to preserve the history and beauty of the area. The park was ultimately taken over by Missouri State Parks and has been a popular destination for St. Louis–area residents ever since. The 2,101-acre Coonville Creek Wild Area provided hideouts during the Civil War as well as during Prohibition. Today the park covers 2,735 acres total and still offers a retreat for visitors looking to get away from the city.

Hiking, camping, boating, fishing, and wading are some of the most popular recreational opportunities in the park. The 110 campsites offer ample space to pitch a tent, take a shower, and even do some laundry. Nearly 18 miles of hiking trails provide plenty of space to get away from the crowds and enjoy nature.

The Mooner's Hollow Trail is a 3-mile loop hike. Named for the moonshining activities that took place in the hollow, the trail travels along Coonville Creek and then up along a rugged ridgeline. Hikers will pass through several glades that offer some brief scenic views and plenty of wildflowers.

From the parking area, locate the information kiosk and trailhead, cross Coonville Creek, and begin hiking northeast, following the obvious trail and blue trail markers. The trail follows Coonville Creek and crosses it at 1.1 miles, then turns to the northwest. After 2.5 miles cross a shallow tributary and continue southwest to the trailhead parking area.

Coonville Creek ▶

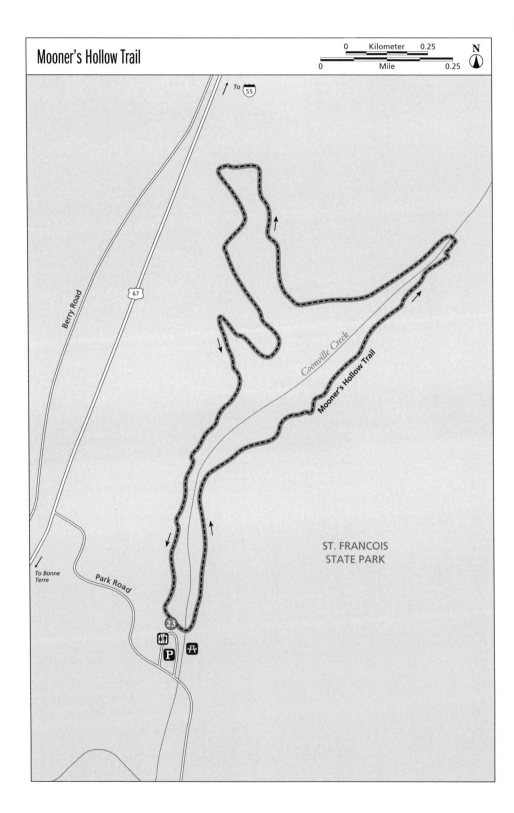

BEING BEAR AWARE

Did you know that there are somewhere between 150 and 300 black bears in Missouri? If you are fortunate enough to encounter a bear, remain watchful. Do not approach the bear. If your presence causes the bear to change its behavior, you're too close. Being too close may promote aggressive behavior from the bear such as running toward you, making loud noises, or swatting the ground. The bear is demanding more space. Do not run. Slowly back away, and keep watching the bear. Try to increase the distance between you and the bear. The bear will probably do the same.

Miles and Directions

0.0 From the trailhead, cross the footbridge and begin hiking northeast.

1.1 Cross Coonville Creek and turn northwest.

2.5 Cross a shallow tributary and continue hiking southwest.

3.0 Arrive back at the trailhead parking area.

GREEN TIP

Keep wildlife wild. Glade reptiles such as the brightly hued collared lizards and the inquisitive fence lizards are part of what make hiking in the Ozarks so special. Sadly, several populations of glade lizards have been decimated due to the illegal collection of these animals as pets. Wild animals do not make good pets. Please leave these incredible creatures in the glades where they can prosper and be enjoyed by everyone.

24 Devils Honeycomb Trail

The Hughes Mountain Natural Area is one of Missouri's geologic wonders. The rock formation here is similar to that of the Devils Tower in Wyoming and the Devils Postpile in California, both national monuments. The short climb to the top is well worth some of the best vistas the state has to offer.

Start: North from trailhead parking area
Distance: 1.7 miles out and back
Hiking time: 1 hour
Difficulty: Moderate due to uphill climb
Trail surface: Dirt packed trail and rock
Best season: Year-round
Other trail users: None
Canine compatibility: Leashed dogs permitted

Land status: Operated by Missouri Department of Conservation
Fees and permits: None
Map: USGS Irondale
Trail contact: Missouri Department of Conservation, Southeast Regional Office, 2302 County Park Dr., Cape Girardeau, MO 63701; (573) 290-5730; https://nature.mdc.mo.gov/discover-nature/places/hughes-mountain

Finding the trailhead: From St. Louis, take I-55 South for 33 miles to exit 174B. From there, take US 67 South for 29 miles before turning right onto MO 8. Drive 4.8 miles and turn left onto Highway M. Continue 8 miles on Highway M until you reach the Missouri Department of Conservation Hughes Mountain Natural Area parking area on the left. **GPS:** N37 48.636' / W90 42.922'

The Hike

Located near Potosi, Missouri, Hughes Mountain Natural Area features a combination of glades, hardwood forests, and unique geologic features. Considered to be one of the state's geologic wonders, the rock outcrops that make up the "honeycomb" design on Hughes Mountain are approximately 1.5 billion years old and are some of the oldest exposed rocks in the United States.

The result of an ancient lava flow, the angular rock formation was created in a way similar to the famous Devils Tower in Wyoming. Also of great natural significance are the area's glades, which contain a variety of native grasses and wildflowers, such as broomsedge, prickly pear cactus, spiderwort, and wild hyacinth. These native grasses and wildflowers provide important habitat for wildlife such as fence lizards and keep the thin, exposed soil from eroding. Once you are on the honeycomb, you will be amazed by the greenish-white lichen that covers much of the rocks' surfaces and forms the most unusual designs.

From the trailhead parking area, begin hiking south through a short section of field that quickly enters a typical Missouri woodland of oaks, maples, and hickories.

Top: Honeycomb rock outcrops on Hughes Mountain ▶
Bottom: Lichen

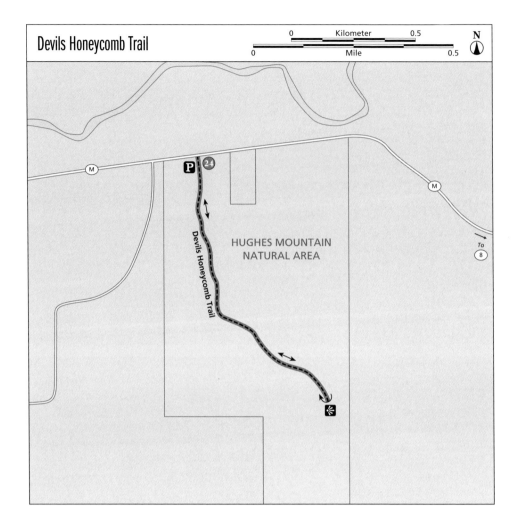

After 0.6 mile you'll reach an opening where the trees and the unique geologic features begin. Navigate your way along the not-so-well-marked trail that leads to the obvious top of Hughes Mountain at 0.85 mile. Return to the trailhead and parking area via the same route at 1.7 miles.

Miles and Directions

0.0 From the Hughes Mountain Natural Area parking area, begin hiking south up Hughes Mountain.

0.6 Reach an opening.

0.85 Reach the top of Hughes Mountain.

1.7 Arrive back at the trailhead parking area.

25 Scour Trail

The Scour Trail at Johnson's Shut-Ins State Park provides access to the scour channel itself, which hikers are allowed to walk down into. The trail also offers views of the Taum Sauk Reservoir. In 2005 the reservoir broke and released a catastrophic flood that almost completely wiped out the park.

Start: South from trailhead parking area
Distance: 2.0 miles out and back with loop
Hiking time: 1.5 hours
Difficulty: Easy due to relatively flat terrain
Trail surface: Dirt packed trail
Best season: Year-round
Other trail users: None
Canine compatibility: Leashed dogs permitted

Land status: Operated by Missouri State Parks
Fees and permits: None
Maps: USGS Johnson's Shut-Ins; trail map available at visitor center
Trail contact: Johnson's Shut-Ins State Park, 148 Taum Sauk Trail, Middlebrook, MO 63656; (573) 546-2450; https://mostateparks.com/trails/johnsons-shut-ins-state-park

Finding the trailhead: From St. Louis, take I-55 South for 33 miles to exit 174B. Exit and continue on US 67 South for 35.6 miles to MO 221. Continue on MO 221 for 7.1 miles and turn right at the fork onto Highway NN. After 9.4 miles turn right onto MO 21 and then left after 0.5 mile onto Highway N. Take Highway N for 12.8 miles before reaching the Scour Trail parking area on the left. **GPS:** N37 33.355' / W90 50.368'

The Hike

Johnson's Shut-Ins State Park is an excellent destination almost any time of year, but it is particularly popular during the hot summer months, when the cool waters of the Black River and the unique rock formations known as shut-ins combine to form the perfect swimming hole. A shut-in is a narrow channel formed by especially hard, erosion-resistant igneous rock. The channels "shut in" the water, forming pools from a few inches to dozens of feet deep, which offer a refreshing retreat during the hot and humid days common to Missouri. In addition to the shut-ins, the area offers hikers, horseback riders, and nature lovers plenty of acres to enjoy the amazing beauty of the Ozarks.

In December 2005 a breach in the Taum Sauk Reservoir unleashed more than one billion gallons of water, ripping trees and soil from the slopes of Proffit Mountain, devastating portions of Johnson's Shut-Ins State Park, and wiping out a large section of the Ozark Trail. In its wake the flood exposed a geological history few could imagine. Uncovering 900 million years of the earth's history, geologists have found both an ancient beach and a mountain range. Several educational and interpretive exhibits have been added to the park to explain the amazing history uncovered by the reservoir breach.

Taum Sauk Reservoir and scour from the Scour Trail

One of the positive outcomes of the reservoir breach is the addition of the Scour Trail, which provides you with an up-close look at the destruction caused by the breach as well as the outstanding history uncovered by its power. The area destroyed by the rushing waters is called the "scour."

From the trailhead parking area, locate the Scour trailhead to the south and hike across the bridge to begin. Come to a fork in the trail at 0.3 mile and stay right (southwest). At 0.6 mile you will reach the Scour Pavilion interpretive site, where you can read about the scour channel. Continue on and pass the Scour Trail loop return at 0.8 mile, then continue to the Slice of Time overlook at 1.0 mile for a view of the Taum Sauk Reservoir.

NEARBY TRAILS

There are several additional trails in Johnson's Shut-Ins State Park, including the 10-mile-long Goggins Mountain Equestrian Trail, the 2.5-mile-long Shut-Ins Trail, and the 1.5-mile-long Horseshoe Glades Trail.

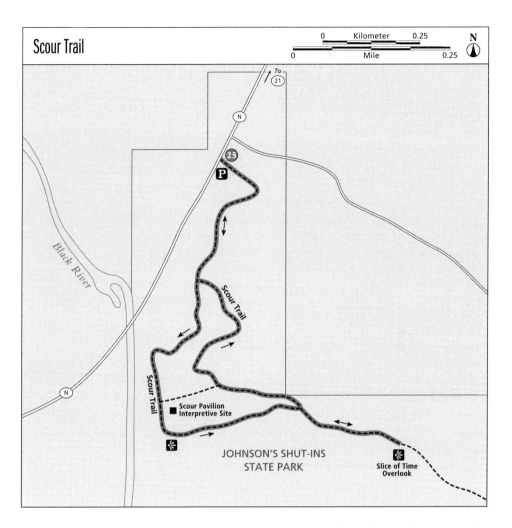

0   Kilometer   0.25

0   Mile   0.25

N

To 21

N

25

P

Black River

Scour Trail

N

Scour Trail

N

Scour Pavilion Interpretive Site

JOHNSON'S SHUT-INS STATE PARK

Slice of Time Overlook

Turn back and reach the Scour Trail loop return on the right (north) at 1.2 miles, and follow the trail northwest until you reach the end of the loop at 1.7 miles. Return to the trailhead at 2.0 miles.

Miles and Directions

0.0 From the Scour Trail parking area, begin hiking south.

0.3 Stay right (southwest) at the fork.

0.6 Come to the Scour Pavilion interpretive site.

0.8 Pass the Scour Trail return loop.

1.0 Reach the Slice of Time overlook, then return to the Scour Trail loop.

1.2 Turn right (north) onto the Scour Trail loop.

1.7 Reach the end of the loop and turn right (north) to return to the trailhead.

2.0 Arrive back at the trailhead.

26 Ozark Trail: Taum Sauk Mountain State Park to Johnson's Shut-Ins State Park

The Ozark Trail is Missouri's version of the Appalachian Trail. As of 2018 many sections of the trail are complete, with a few sections still under construction. The section of trail from Taum Sauk Mountain State Park to Johnson's Shut-Ins State Park is considered by many to be the best portion of the trail. This section offers rugged terrain, the highest point in the state, and beautiful scenery.

Start: Southwest from the Mina Sauk Falls trailhead in Taum Sauk Mountain State Park
Distance: 13.2-mile shuttle
Hiking time: 8 to 9 hours
Difficulty: Difficult due to rugged trail and length
Trail surface: Dirt packed trail
Best season: Spring through fall
Other trail users: None
Canine compatibility: Leashed dogs permitted

Land status: Operated by Missouri State Parks and Ozark Trail Association
Fees and permits: None
Maps: USGS Ironton; Ozark Trail–Taum Sauk Section map available at trailhead
Trail contact: Johnson's Shut-Ins State Park, 148 Taum Sauk Trail, Middlebrook, MO 63656; (573) 546-2450; https://mostateparks.com/trails/johnsons-shut-ins-state-park

Finding the trailhead: From St. Louis, take I-55 South for 33 miles to exit 174B. Exit and continue on US 67 South for 35.6 miles to MO 221. Continue on MO 221 for 7.1 miles and turn left to stay on MO 221 for another 8.9 miles. Turn left onto MO 21 and drive 6.9 miles to Highway CC and the signed turn for Taum Sauk Mountain State Park. Turn right onto Highway CC and continue 3.6 miles to the parking area. **GPS:** N37 34.369'/W90 43.700'

The Hike

With nearly 400 miles of mostly linked trail sections, the Ozark Trail is the premier backpacking destination in Missouri. Future plans for the trail have it reaching from St. Louis to the Arkansas border, and then linking with the Ozark Highland Trail in Arkansas to create a 700-mile trail and through-hiker paradise. Deer, turkeys, bobcats, bears, and bald eagles are just a few of the wild animals that you may encounter while hiking over the rugged hills of the Ozarks.

At 1,772 feet, Taum Sauk Mountain is the highest point in the state of Missouri. Many consider the 13.2 miles of the Ozark Trail between Taum Sauk Mountain State Park and Johnson's Shut-Ins State Park to be the most rugged section of the entire trail. This stretch is best done as a shuttle, but can be done as an out-and-back trip for hikers looking to spend several days in the area.

In December 2005 a breach in the Taum Sauk Reservoir unleashed more than one billion gallons of water, ripping trees and soil from the slopes of Proffit Mountain,

Ozark Trail

devastating portions of Johnson's Shut-Ins State Park and wiping out a large section of the Ozark Trail. The massive flood uncovered a geological history few could imagine. Approximately 900 million years of the earth's history was uncovered, exposing both an ancient beach and a mountain range. Several educational and interpretive exhibits have been added to the park to explain the amazing history uncovered by the reservoir breach.

From the Taum Sauk Mountain parking area, locate the Mina Sauk Falls Loop trailhead at the southwest corner. Begin hiking southwest on the trail and reach a fork in the trail at 0.2 mile. Proceeding left will take you to the Missouri high point. Instead, continue right (southwest) to a second fork at 0.3 mile. Avoid the Mina Sauk Falls Loop return trail on the left, instead staying right (southwest) as the trail becomes more rocky and rugged and descends slightly. Reach the junction of the Mina Sauk Falls Loop Trail and Ozark Trail at 1.4 miles and bear right (southwest) onto the Ozark Trail.

The trail makes a steep descent down to the base of Mina Sauk Falls at 1.6 miles and continues on to the Devils Tollgate at 2.4 miles. The trail climbs up above the valley floor and Taum Sauk Creek. (Perhaps to keep hikers higher in case of another reservoir disaster?) At 5.5 miles the trail makes a sharp left (south) turn and begins a

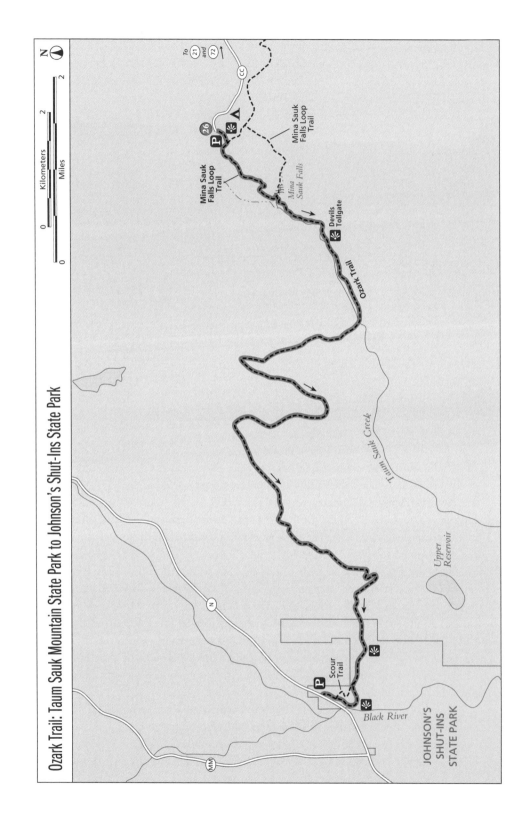

Ozark Trail: Taum Sauk Mountain State Park to Johnson's Shut-Ins State Park

N

Kilometers
0   2

Miles
0   2

To 21 and 72

CC

26

P

Mina Sauk Falls Loop Trail

Mina Sauk Falls Loop Trail

Mina Sauk Falls Loop Trail

Mina Sauk Falls

Devils Tollgate

Ozark Trail

Taum Sauk Creek

N

Upper Reservoir

Scour Trail

P

Black River

JOHNSON'S SHUT-INS STATE PARK

MM

steady ascent to a great view of the Ozarks and Taum Sauk Reservoir at 6.3 miles. Take in the views and continue north to Proffit Mountain.

At 10.7 miles hikers will pass an unnamed overlook to the left (south) and then a sign for Johnson's Shut-Ins State Park at 11.7 miles indicating that the park is 1.5 miles away. The Ozark Trail connects with the Scour Trail at 12.2 miles and continues west to 12.4 miles, where hikers stay left on the Ozark Trail / Scour Trail. Keep left (north) again at the fork in the trail at 12.9 miles to stay on the Ozark Trail and reach the Scour Trail parking area at 13.2 miles.

Miles and Directions

0.0 Begin hiking southwest from the Mina Sauk Falls Loop trailhead at Taum Sauk Mountain State Park.

0.2 Come to a fork in the trail and turn right (northwest). Going left will take you to the highest point in Missouri.

0.3 Reach a second fork and the trailhead register point. Stay right (southwest) again toward Mina Sauk Falls.

1.4 The Mina Sauk Falls Loop Trail connects with the Ozark Trail. Left (east) will lead to Mina Sauk Falls and continue on the loop. For now, turn right (southwest) onto the Ozark Trail toward the Devils Tollgate and follow the white-and-green OT blazes.

1.6 Pass the base of Mina Sauk Falls.

2.4 Reach the Devils Tollgate and continue hiking southwest.

5.5 The trail makes a sharp turn south and begins a steady ascent.

6.3 Taum Sauk Reservoir is viewable to the south.

10.7 Reach an unnamed overlook to the left (south).

11.7 Come to a sign for Johnson's Shut-Ins State Park, indicating it is 1.5 miles away.

12.2 The Ozark Trail connects with the Scour Trail.

12.4 Stay left (west) on the Ozark Trail. The trail to the right is the Scour Trail loop.

12.9 Reach a fork and turn left (north). Right is the Scour Trail loop.

13.2 Reach the Scour Trail parking area in Johnson's Shut-Ins State Park.

27 Mina Sauk Falls Loop Trail / Ozark Trail to Devils Tollgate

Taum Sauk Mountain State Park boasts both Missouri's highest point and the state's tallest waterfall. A visit to the high point first, then Mina Sauk Falls, followed by a hike down to the Devils Tollgate rock formation makes this hike a nice little trifecta.

Start: Southwest from the Mina Sauk Falls trailhead parking area
Distance: 5.1 miles out and back with loop
Hiking time: 3 hours
Difficulty: Difficult due to steep climb and rugged terrain
Trail surface: Dirt packed trail and rock
Best seasons: Spring and fall
Other trail users: None

Canine compatibility: Leashed dogs permitted
Land status: Operated by Missouri State Parks
Fees and permits: None
Maps: USGS Ironton; Ozark Trail–Taum Sauk Section map available at trailhead
Trail contact: Johnson's Shut-Ins State Park, 148 Taum Sauk Trail, Middlebrook, MO 63656; (573) 546-2450; https://mostateparks.com/trails/taum-sauk-mountain-state-park

Finding the trailhead: From St. Louis, take I-55 South for 33 miles to exit 174B. Exit and continue on US 67 South for 35.6 miles to MO 221. Continue on MO 221 for 7.1 miles and turn left to stay on MO 221 for another 8.9 miles. Turn left onto MO 21 and drive 6.9 miles to Highway CC and the signed turn for Taum Sauk Mountain State Park. Turn right onto Highway CC and continue 3.6 miles to the parking area. **GPS:** N37 34.369' / W90 43.700'

The Hike

Located in the St. Francois Mountains, Taum Sauk Mountain State Park is one of the most rugged and beautiful locations in the state. Formed more than one billion years ago, this area was created when volcanic eruptions of hot ash settled and cooled to form rhyolite.

Traces of these mountains still remain, although they are now covered in hardwood forests of oak and hickory. The highest point in Missouri, Taum Sauk Mountain's elevation is 1,772 feet. This rugged day hike leads you past the highest point and the tallest wet-weather waterfall in the state. You will also be on part of the longest trail in the state, the 392-mile-long Ozark Trail. The turnaround point for this hike is Devils Tollgate, a hunk of volcanic rhyolite that stands more than 30 feet tall.

From the Taum Sauk Mountain parking area, locate the Mina Sauk Falls Loop trailhead at the southwest corner of the parking area. Begin hiking southwest on the trail and reach a fork at 0.2 mile. (The spur trail to the left goes to the Missouri high point.) Stay right for a short distance, coming to the trailhead register at 0.3 mile, where the trail forks again. Stay right (northwest) to begin the loop portion of the hike. The trail becomes more rocky and rugged and descends slightly on the way to

Devils Tollgate

OZARK TRAIL TRIVIA

The Ozark Trail is marked with green-and-white OT trail markers. They are typically attached to trees vertically. If you see an OT trail marker attached to a tree at an angle, it indicates a major turn in the trail.

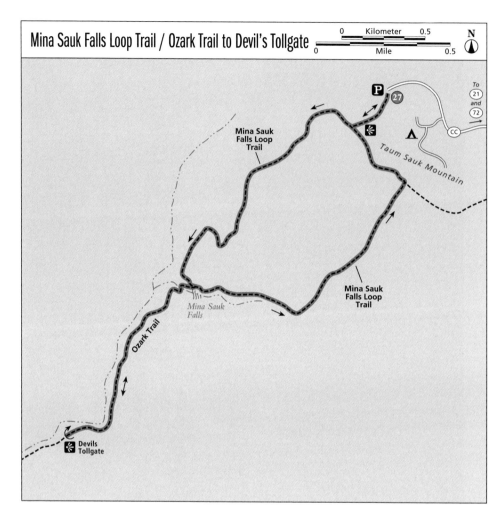

Mina Sauk Falls. Reach the junction of the Mina Sauk Falls Loop Trail and Ozark Trail at 1.4 miles and bear right (southwest) onto the Ozark Trail.

The trail makes a steep descent down to the base of Mina Sauk Falls at 1.6 miles and continues on to the Devils Tollgate at 2.4 miles. After a few pictures, return to the Mina Sauk Falls Loop Trail / Ozark Trail junction and turn right (east) to continue past the falls and keep hiking the loop. Reach a fork at 4.5 miles where the Mina Sauk Falls Loop Trail leads to the left (northwest) and continues on to the trailhead

LIGHTEN YOUR LOAD

After each hiking trip, take a look at the gear you brought and make notes on what you did and did not use. From there, you can start eliminating unused items.

Eastern collared lizard near Mina Sauk Falls

register at 4.8 miles. Turn right (northeast) at the fork and reach another fork at 4.9 miles, where hikers will stay left (northeast) to return to the trailhead.

Miles and Directions

0.0   Begin hiking southwest from the Mina Sauk Falls Loop trailhead at Taum Sauk Mountain State Park.

0.2   Come to a fork in the trail and stay right (northwest). Going left will take you to the highest point in Missouri.

0.3   Reach a second fork and the trailhead register. Stay right (southwest), again toward Mina Sauk Falls.

1.4   The Mina Sauk Falls Loop Trail connects with the Ozark Trail. A left (east) turn will lead to Mina Sauk Falls and continue on the loop. For now, turn right (southwest) onto the Ozark Trail toward the Devil's Tollgate and follow the white-and-green OT blazes.

1.6   Pass the base of Mina Sauk Falls.

2.4   Reach the Devils Tollgate, then return to Mina Sauk Falls.

3.4   Return to the Mina Sauk Falls Loop Trail and Ozark Trail junction. Turn right (east) to continue on the Mina Sauk Falls Loop Trail and the Ozark Trail.

4.5   Reach the second Ozark Trail and Mina Sauk Falls Loop Trail junction. Turn left (northwest) to complete the Mina Sauk Falls Loop Trail.

4.8   Return to the trailhead register and turn right (northeast).

4.9   Return to the first fork and stay right (northeast).

5.1   Arrive back at the trailhead.

28 Trail through Time

A highlight of the Pickle Springs Natural Area, this short interpretive hike features towering limestone bluffs, breezy canyons, and several interesting rock formations.

Start: East from trailhead parking area
Distance: 2-mile loop
Hiking time: 1 to 2 hours
Difficulty: Moderate due to modest climb
Trail surface: Dirt packed trail
Best season: Year-round
Other trail users: None
Canine compatibility: Leashed dogs permitted

Land status: Operated by Missouri Department of Conservation
Fees and permits: None
Maps: USGS Sprott; interpretive trail guide available at information kiosk
Trail contact: Pickle Springs Natural Area, 2302 County Park Dr., Cape Girardeau, MO 63701; (573) 290-5730; https://nature.mdc.mo.gov/discover-nature/places/pickle-springs

Finding the trailhead: From St. Louis, take I-55 South for 57 miles to MO 32 at exit 150. Follow MO 32 west from the I-55 junction past Hawn State Park to CR AA. Turn left onto CR AA and drive about 1 mile to Dorlac Road. Turn left and follow the gravel Dorlac Road about 0.5 mile to the parking lot and trailhead located on the right. **GPS:** N37 48.083' / W90 18.087'

The Hike

Pickle Springs Natural Area received its name from Illinois settler William Pickles in the 1850s. Over time, as more has been learned about the area, it has received more and more recognition. The area was designated a National Natural Landmark in 1974 and is also a State Natural Area.

Researchers believe that mammoths once roamed the canyons here, grazing on plants like northern white violets, orchids, and cinnamon ferns. All of these plants can still be found in Pickle Springs Natural Area. It tends to be the geology that keeps visitors coming back, though, and the Trail through Time highlights some of the area's most unusual rock formations. The LaMotte sandstone has made its way from the bottom of ancient seas to expose rock formations not typically seen in Missouri.

The Trail through Time is a 2-mile loop hike. The interpretive trail has been designed to lead hikers through all of the area's amazing sites. Hikers will have the opportunity to enjoy beautiful rock formations, cool box canyons, and a lush forest. Some visitors will find that the 2-mile hike takes longer than an hour because of all the sites.

From the parking area, begin hiking east on the obvious and well-maintained mulch trail. At 0.1 mile come to the information kiosk, which is stocked with trail maps and an interpretive pamphlet that corresponds to many of the sites along the

Double Arch

trail. The loop begins at the kiosk. Turn left (north) to continue on the one-way trail.

At 0.2 mile come to the hallway-like rock formation known as the Slot. Turn right (east) and walk between the tight walls of LaMotte sandstone. Arrive at the more interesting rock formations known as Cauliflower Rocks and pass through

READY-FOR-ANYTHING GEAR LIST

Carry these ten items with you and be prepared for any surprises that Mother Nature may dish out:

1) map and compass

2) sun protection

3) layers of clothing

4) flashlight

5) first-aid kit

6) fire starter

7) extra food

8) extra water

9) shelter

10) knife

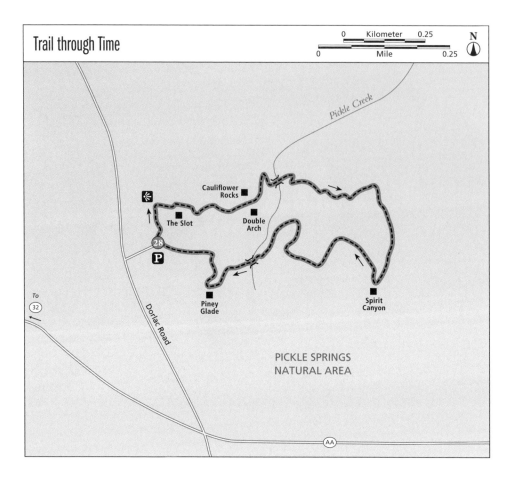

the Double Arch at 0.4 mile. At 0.6 mile you'll come to a wooden footbridge and continue northeast across Pickle Creek. Come to the bluff shelter, known as Spirit Canyon, at 1.0 mile and follow the trail as it curves to the right (west). Cross Pickle Creek again at 1.5 miles and continue west. At 1.7 miles come to Piney Glade, a sandstone glade, near the top of the ridge and follow the trail as it curves to the northwest. At 1.9 miles return to the information kiosk, turn left (west), and return to the parking area.

Miles and Directions

0.0 Begin hiking east on the obvious mulch trail.

0.1 Turn left (north) at the information kiosk.

0.2 Pass through the Slot.

0.4 Pass by Cauliflower Rocks and through the Double Arch.

0.6 Cross Pickle Creek and continue northeast.

1.0 Come to Spirit Canyon and begin heading west.

1.5 Cross Pickle Creek and continue west.

1.7 Come to Piney Glade and follow the trail as it curves to the northeast.

1.9 Return to the information kiosk and turn left (west).

2.0 Arrive back at the trailhead parking area.

HIKING WITH KIDS

We are confident that children will enjoy the Trail through Time at Pickle Springs Natural Area. The strange rock formations and gurgling springs will enchant kids and adults alike. To make the most out of this family-friendly day hike, consider the following tips before leaving home:

- Check the local weather conditions. Adults may not mind hiking in the wind, rain, or cold, but young children will enjoy the hike more if they are comfortable. Pack extra clothing just in case.

- Depending on the age of your children, you should lengthen the amount of time it will take you to complete the hike. For young children, plan on doubling or tripling the time it would take an adult to finish the hike. You will want to leave lots of time to explore, snack, and rest.

- Bring plenty of sunscreen, bug repellent, snacks, and water. Remember a comfortable child makes for a happy hiker.

- Don't expect older children to be excited about hiking for the sake of hiking. Choose hikes that have a destination. Be ready to answer the question, "Why are we hiking here?" Kids will be much more motivated to hike if you give them an interesting destination.

For more tips on hiking with your kids, check out the FalconGuide *Hiking with Kids* by Robin Tawney Nichols.

29 White Oaks Trail

Winding through a mixed hardwood forest, the White Oaks Trail features mature white oaks and lofty shortleaf pines, as well as the unusual outcroppings of LaMotte sandstone.

Start: Trailhead parking area
Distance: 4.1-mile lollipop
Hiking time: 2 to 3 hours
Difficulty: Moderate due to length
Trail surface: Dirt packed trail
Best season: Year-round
Other trail users: None
Canine compatibility: Leashed dogs permitted

Land status: Operated by Missouri State Parks
Fees and permits: None
Maps: USGS Coffman Quad; trail maps available at visitor center
Trail contact: Hawn State Park, 12096 Park Dr., Ste. Genevieve, MO 63670; (573) 883-3603; https://mostateparks.com/park/hawn-state-park

Finding the trailhead: From St. Louis, take I-55 South for 57 miles to exit 150. Turn right onto MO 32 toward the town of Farmington. After 11.3 miles turn left onto MO 144 and drive south for 2.9 miles to the Hawn State Park entrance. At the park entrance turn right into the White Oaks Trail parking area. **GPS:** N37 49.997' / W90 14.415'

The Hike

Boasting some of the most scenic views in the state, Hawn State Park offers a wonderfully diverse natural landscape, with canyon-rimmed valleys, clear sand-bottom streams, and mixed oak-pine forests. Large stands of mature shortleaf pine, Missouri's only native pine species, are one of the park's many highlights that can be easily enjoyed from the White Oaks Trail. Another natural jewel to notice on this hike is the LaMotte sandstone. This ancient, coarse-grained sandstone has the ability to hold groundwater and produces a variety of distinctive flowers and plants.

From the parking area, locate the trailhead register and information kiosk and follow the obvious and well-marked White Oaks Trail west as it gradually descends through a shortleaf pine forest before crossing a small, shallow creek. Shortly after crossing this creek, Connector Trail #1 branches to the left (southeast). This trail, marked with a yellow arrow, takes you to the Whispering Pines Trail. Continue west to stay on the White Oaks Trail, as it crosses another shallow creek and heads up a mellow ridge through a mixed hardwood forest and LaMotte sandstone outcroppings.

After 1.1 miles Connector Trail #2 branches to the left (southeast). Follow the sign pointing toward the White Oaks Trail and cross another shallow creek. You will soon come to a sign that reads "White Oaks Trail Loop 1.8 Miles" with an arrow pointing to the right. Follow this loop trail north, then west, as it follows the sandy

JD at the White Oaks Trail trailhead

drainage, where wildlife tracks are easily visible. Complete the loop portion of the hike at 2.9 miles and return to the trailhead following the same trail.

TICK REMOVAL 101

Missouri and southern Illinois tend to have some heavy tick seasons. If you don't catch them right away and they have time to attach to your skin, follow these directions: 1) Using tweezers, grasp the tick firmly at its head or mouth near your skin, 2) pull firmly and steadily until the tick releases its grip, 3) dispose of the tick as you see fit, 4) swab the bite with alcohol.

White Oaks Trail

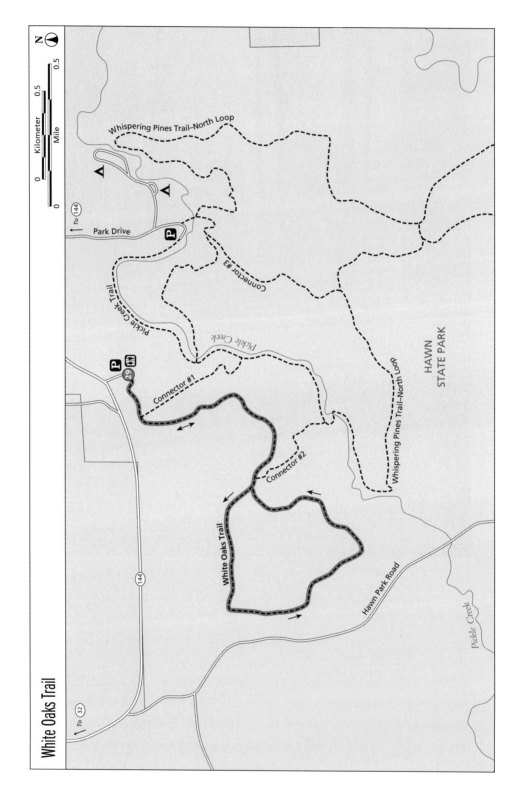

Whispering Pines Trail–North Loop

Connector #3

Park Drive

To 144

Pickle Creek Trail

Connector #1

Pickle Creek

Connector #2

White Oaks Trail

Whispering Pines Trail–North Loop

HAWN STATE PARK

Hawn Park Road

Pickle Creek

To 32

144

N

Kilometer
0   0.5

Mile
0   0.5

Shortleaf pine tree

Miles and Directions

0.0 Leave the parking area and begin hiking west on the White Oaks Trail.

0.2 Connector Trail #1 branches to the left (southeast); continue straight on the White Oaks Trail.

1.1 Connector Trail #2 branches to the left (southeast); follow the signs pointing toward the White Oaks Trail.

1.2 Reach the beginning of the White Oaks Trail loop and bear right (northwest).

2.9 Come to the end of the White Oaks Trail loop, turn right (east), and return to the trailhead via the same route.

4.1 Arrive back at the trailhead.

30 Whispering Pines Trail–North Loop

A 6.5-mile loop through a mixed hardwood and pine forest, the north loop of the Whispering Pines Trail offers a longer day trip for hikers looking to take in many of the sites in Hawn State Park.

Start: South from the Whispering Pines trailhead parking area
Distance: 6.5-mile loop
Hiking time: 4 hours
Difficulty: Difficult due to length and some challenging climbs
Trail surface: Dirt packed trail
Best season: Fall through spring
Other trail users: None

Canine compatibility: Leashed dogs permitted
Land status: Operated by Missouri State Parks
Fees and permits: None
Maps: USGS Coffman; trail maps available at visitor center
Trail contact: Hawn State Park, 12096 Park Dr., Ste. Genevieve, MO 63670; (573) 883-3603, https://mostateparks.com/park/hawn-state-park

Finding the trailhead: From St. Louis, take I-55 South for 57 miles to MO 32 West at exit 150. Follow MO 32 west from the I-55 junction for 11.3 miles to MO 144. Turn left onto MO 144 and follow the road for 2.9 miles to the park entrance. At the stop sign turn left onto Park Drive and continue 1.1 miles to a fork. Stay right at the fork and drive 0.1 mile to the parking area and trailhead on the left. **GPS:** N37 49.760' / W90 13.811'

The Hike

Many visitors who come to Hawn State Park believe it to be the loveliest park in Missouri. The 4,953-acre park is located in the eastern Ozark Mountains and is home to the 2,880-acre Whispering Pine Wild Area and Pickle Creek, a State Natural Area. The park was acquired by the state in 1955.

The area is believed to have been part of a large, sandy floodplain around 600 million years ago, which stretched as far north as Canada. Through cycles of uplift and erosion, the sandstone cliffs and bluffs are what remain. Today hikers can enjoy rich shortleaf pine forests, mixed oak and maple trees, and plenty of flowering dogwoods. The park is also popular with rock hounds and birders.

The Whispering Pines North Loop Trail is a 6.5-mile loop hike. On a windy day a hiker will learn why the trail is called the Whispering Pines Trail. Many people say it sounds like the pine trees are actually whispering to you as the wind blows through them. For an extended hike or even a short, overnight backpack trip, the north loop can be combined with the south loop for a 10-mile hike.

From the parking area, locate the Whispering Pines Trail to the south. There is a sign marking the trail at the trailhead, and hikers are encouraged to sign in at the

Whispering Pines Trail ▶

Whispering Pines Trail–North Loop

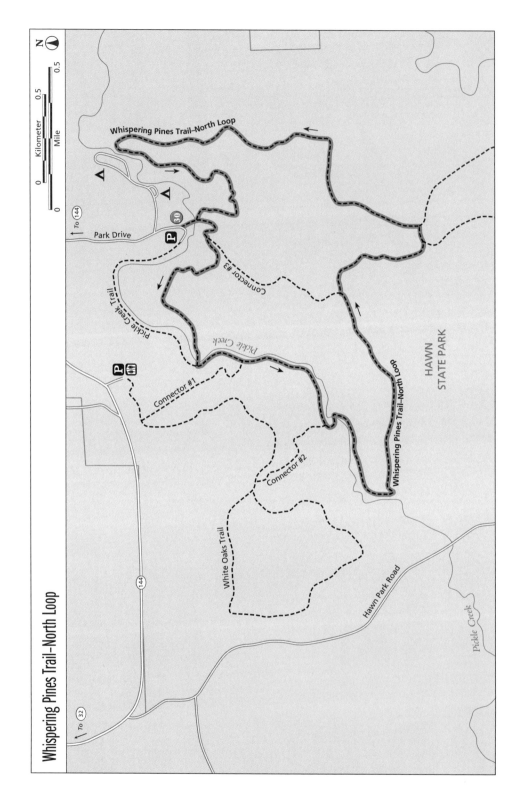

Whispering Pines Trail–North Loop

Whispering Pines Trail–North Loop

Pickle Creek Trail

Connector #3

Connector #1

Connector #2

White Oaks Trail

Park Drive

To 144

Pickle Creek

Pickle Creek

Pickle Creek

HAWN STATE PARK

Hawn Park Road

To 32

144

30

N

Kilometer

Mile

0.5

0.5

0

0

trailhead register. Cross the wooden footbridge and continue hiking south to cross a second wooden footbridge at 0.1 mile. Turn right here and follow the red directional arrow southwest.

At 0.3 mile you'll come to a fork in the trail. Stay right (southwest) to stay on the Whispering Pines Trail–North Loop. Wade across the babbling Pickle Creek at 1.0 mile and turn left (west). Come to Connector Trail #1, which connects to the White Oaks Trail, at 1.3 miles, stay left, and continue hiking southwest on the Whispering Pines Trail–North Loop. At 1.8 miles come to Connector Trail #2, which also connects to the White Oaks Trail; stay left and continue southwest.

At 3.2 miles arrive at Connector Trail #3 on the left (north) side of the trail, which leads to a primitive camping area and can be used to shorten this hike, as it eventually leads to the trailhead parking area. Stay right (east) to continue on the Whispering Pines Trail–North Loop. At 3.7 miles come to the junction of the Whispering Pines Trail–North Loop and the Whispering Pines Trail–South Loop. Stay to the left (northeast) to continue on the north loop.

After another 0.1 mile come to a second junction with the south loop. Again, stay left (north) to continue on the north loop and return to the trailhead. Come to Pickle Creek at 5.4 miles and follow the trail as it turns to the left (southwest). At 6.4 miles return to the footbridge, turn right (north) to cross the bridge, and return to the trailhead parking area.

Miles and Directions

0.0 Begin hiking south, crossing a wooden footbridge.

0.1 Cross a second wooden footbridge and turn right (southwest).

0.3 Come to a fork in the trail, stay right, and continue southwest.

1.0 Cross Pickle Creek and turn left (west).

1.3 Avoid Connector Trail #1.

1.8 Avoid Connector Trail #2.

3.2 Avoid Connector Trail #3 and continue east.

3.7 Avoid the Whispering Pines Trail-South Loop and continue northeast.

3.8 Stay left (north) at the second junction with the Whispering Pines Trail-South Loop.

5.4 Arrive at Pickle Creek. The trail turns to the left (southwest).

6.4 Return to the wooden footbridge, turn right (north) to cross the bridge, and return to the trailhead parking area.

6.5 Arrive back at the trailhead.

JD and Arnie taking a break on the Whispering Pines Trail

JD'S FAMOUS TRAIL MIX RECIPE

One of our favorite mixes that we make at home comes from products we buy at the local natural foods store:

2 cups salted cashews (JD likes honey roasted)

1 cup raw macadamia nuts

1 cup dried pineapple

1 cup dried cranberries (JD likes orange flavored)

1 cup dried mango

1 cup Nature's Path granola (optional)

31 Sheppard Point Trail

This exceptional day hike offers steep inclines and scenic ridgetop views of the Mississippi River. The quick out-and-back hike lets hikers experience the rolling hills of the Ozarks and the beauty of the mighty Mississippi.

Start: Sheppard Point trailhead parking area
Distance: 3 miles out and back
Hiking time: 2 hours
Difficulty: Moderate due to steep climbs
Trail surface: Dirt packed trail
Best season: Year-round
Other trail users: None
Canine compatibility: Leashed dogs permitted

Land status: Operated by Missouri State Parks
Fees and permits: None
Maps: USGS Ware; trail maps available at visitor center
Trail contact: Trail of Tears State Park, 429 Moccasin Springs Rd., Jackson, MO 63755; (573) 334-1711; https://mostateparks.com/trails/trail-tears-state-park?type=hiking

Finding the trailhead: From St. Louis, take I-55 South for 102 miles to exit 105 toward Fruitland. Turn left (east) onto US 61 North / High Street and drive 1.1 miles to MO 177. Turn right (east) onto MO 177 and continue 7.4 miles to a stop sign. Turn right (south) to stay on MO 177 and drive 4.1 miles to the park entrance. Turn left (northeast) onto Moccasin Springs Road and drive 0.3 mile before passing the visitor center on the left. Continue another 0.8 mile to the Greensferry Shelter / Sheppard Point trailhead on the right. **GPS:** N37 26.697' / W89 28.007'

The Hike

Trail of Tears State Park offers some of the best day hikes in southeast Missouri. Rich in both natural and cultural history, the park makes an excellent weekend destination and is a relatively short distance from St. Louis thanks to the direct route that I-55 offers.

The park's name hints at one of America's darkest chapters. The Indian Removal Act of 1830 set the stage for the relocation of Native Americans living east of the Mississippi River. Many tribes were affected by the act, including members of the Cherokee, Choctaw, Chickasaw, Creek, and Seminole nations. Trail of Tears State Park honors the relocation of the Cherokee. During the winter of 1838–39, more than 16,000 Cherokee were forced to relocate from their homelands in and around western North Carolina to Indian Territory, which is in present-day Oklahoma. The 1,000-mile journey took the lives of more than 4,000 people along the way and came to be known as the Trail of Tears. The park's visitor center offers an excellent interpretation of this tragic event and is well worth a visit.

Positioned on the banks of the mighty Mississippi River, this state park is a prime location for viewing migrating waterfowl, including several species of ducks. The Sheppard Point Trail is also a prime location to spot eagles, particularly in winter.

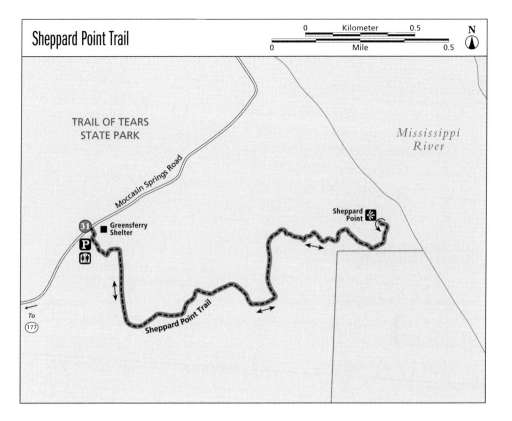

Sheppard Point Trail

TRAIL OF TEARS
STATE PARK

Moccasin Springs Road

Mississippi
River

Sheppard
Point

31

Greensferry
Shelter

P

To
177

Sheppard Point Trail

0   Kilometer   0.5

0   Mile   0.5

N

The Sheppard Point Trail is located at the Greensferry Shelter on Moccasin Springs Road. From the trailhead, begin hiking southeast on the obvious and well-marked dirt path and cross the footbridge. The trail quickly begins to ascend a steep ridge through the hardwood woodland of mostly oak and hickory trees. At 0.2 mile you'll reach a ridgeline and the trail continues uphill along this ridge. After hiking uphill for 0.9 mile, the trail makes a sharp left (east) turn and gradually begins going downhill. From here, continue hiking east on the trail.

At 1.1 miles you'll come to a bench; stay right (southeast) on the trail. Beyond the bench (to the left) you'll notice an old path that park employees are working to cover up. This is a portion of the old Sheppard Point Trail. The original trail took on a large amount of storm damage a few years back, causing the park managers to reroute a large section of the trail.

As you continue downhill from the bench, the trail gets a bit more rocky and rugged before reaching a creek crossing at 1.3 miles. Look for beech, poplar, and magnolia trees as you hike through this valley before climbing another steep ridge that takes you to Sheppard Point at 1.5 miles from the trailhead. This bluff offers one of the best views in the park. Keep an eye on both the sky and the ground at this

◀ *Sheppard Point Trail in winter*

point, as we have spotted both eagles and timber rattlesnakes on this portion of the trail. After taking in the views of the mighty Mississippi River at Sheppard Point, turn around and return to the trailhead via the same route.

Miles and Directions

0.0 From the trailhead register, begin hiking southeast.

0.2 Reach a ridgeline and continue hiking uphill

0.9 The trail makes a sharp left (east) turn and gradually begins going downhill.

1.1 Come to a bench; stay right (southeast) on the trail.

1.5 Reach Sheppard Point (overlook).

3.0 Arrive back at the trailhead.

BUSHYHEAD MEMORIAL

Located northeast of the Greensferry Shelter and the Sheppard Point trailhead is the Bushyhead Memorial. The memorial pays tribute to Nancy Bushyhead Walker Hildebrand. She was the sister of Reverend Jesse Bushyhead and the wife of Lewis Hildebrand, both of whom led Cherokee detachments through Cape Girardeau County. Legend has it that she died and was buried within the park's boundaries. The memorial honors her and all the Cherokee who died on the trail.

32 Lake Trail

This easy day hike follows the shoreline of Lake Boutin and is easily accessible from the campground.

Start: Southwest corner of trailhead parking area
Distance: 2.25-mile lollipop
Hiking time: 1 hour
Difficulty: Easy
Trail surface: Dirt packed trail
Best season: Year-round
Other trail users: None
Canine compatibility: Leashed dogs permitted

Land status: Operated by Missouri State Parks
Fees and permits: None
Maps: USGS Ware; trail maps available at visitor center
Trail contact: Trail of Tears State Park, 429 Moccasin Springs Rd., Jackson, MO 63755; (573) 334-1711; https://mostateparks.com/trails/trail-tears-state-park?type=hiking

Finding the trailhead: From St. Louis, take I-55 South for 102 miles to exit 105 toward Fruitland. Turn left (east) onto US 61 North / High Street and drive 1.1 miles to MO 177. Turn right (east) onto MO 177 and continue 7.4 miles to a stop sign. Turn right (south) to stay on MO 177 and drive 2.9 miles to the park entrance. Turn left (north) onto Hill Road and drive 0.5 mile to the parking area on the right. **GPS: N37 27.293' / W89 29.101'**

The Hike

Rich in both natural and cultural history, Trail of Tears State Park makes an excellent weekend destination and is a relatively short distance from St. Louis thanks to the direct route that I-55 offers. The park gets its name from the tragic Cherokee relocation known as the Trail of Tears, which came through Jackson, Missouri, in the winter of 1838–39. Thousands of Native Americans died on this journey. Visit the park's visitor center to learn more about this dark chapter of American history.

Positioned on the banks of the mighty Mississippi River, this state park offers lush hardwood woodlands and towering bluff-top views, as well as hiking, camping, and fishing opportunities. The Lake Trail is an easy day hike that takes visitors along the shore of Lake Boutin, over several ridges, and through the basic camping area. Be on the lookout for the rare pennywort, which can be found growing near the trail in the early spring.

WILD WEATHER

The trails at Trail of Tears State Park have endured a lot over the years. Recent ice storms and an "inland hurricane" devastated the trails throughout the park. Efforts by the Missouri Youth Conservation Corps have reopened the trails.

Lake Boutin

The trailhead is located about 100 yards from the southwest corner of the parking area. From the trailhead, the obvious dirt trail follows the lakeshore for 0.2 mile. At 0.2 mile come to the beginning of the loop portion of the hike. Take the left fork of the trail and hike southeast toward the basic campground. At 0.4 mile come to the park road. Turn left (east) onto the road and follow it for 0.1 mile, after which the trail continues southeast on the opposite side of the road. Be on the lookout for hints of the area's past, such as the remnants of an old homestead, old barbed-wire fence, and a man-made pond.

At 1.9 miles pass a campsite, stay left, and continue hiking northwest for about 0.1 mile to the lakeshore. At 2.0 miles turn right (east) and follow the lakeshore. At 2.1

SNAKEBITES!

The best advice we can give here is, don't get bitten. The best way to avoid a snakebite is to watch where you are putting your hands and feet. If you do get bitten, though, the best thing to do is to get to a hospital for some antivenom. Forget all the debunked and unproven methods of the "cut and suck," tourniquets, and suction devices. Simply clean the bitten area with an alcohol swab, remove the person's backpack and any restrictive clothing and/or jewelry near the bitten area, and walk (or carry if possible) him or her off the trail. Knowing what kind of snake bit the hiker will be a huge help at the hospital.

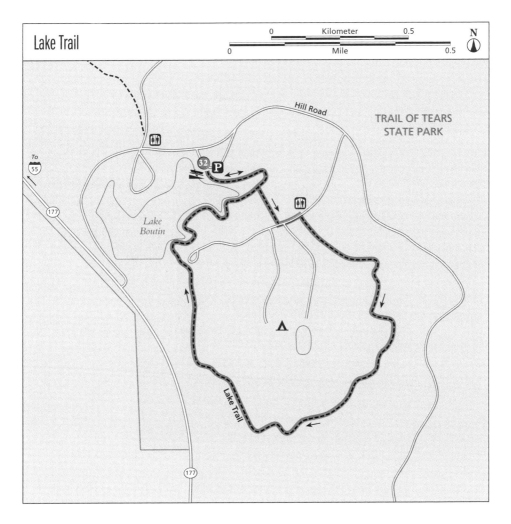

0   Kilometer   0.5

0   Mile   0.5

N

Hill Road

TRAIL OF TEARS
STATE PARK

To
55

177

Lake
Boutin

Lake Trail

177

miles complete the loop section of the hike. Stay left and follow the trail northeast back to the trailhead and parking area.

Miles and Directions

0.0 From the trailhead, follow the obvious dirt path east as it hugs the lakeshore.

0.2 At the beginning of the loop portion of the hike, turn left (southeast).

0.4 At the campground road, turn left and follow the road east.

0.5 The trail resumes on the opposite side of the road; continue hiking southeast.

1.9 Pass a campsite and picnic table; stay left and continue hiking northwest.

2.0 Reach the shore of Lake Boutin and turn right (east).

2.1 At the end of the loop portion of the hike, stay left (northeast) to return to the trailhead and parking area.

2.25 Arrive back at the trailhead and parking area.

33 Pee-Wah Trail

The 8.5-mile Pee-Wah Trail winds through the Indian Creek Wild Area and can be done as a longer day hike or made into an overnight trip. This trail will get you out into the more remote parts of Trail of Tears State Park.

Start: Northwest corner of parking area
Distance: 8.5-mile lollipop with double loop
Hiking time: 4 to 5 hours
Difficulty: Difficult due to length and terrain
Trail surface: Dirt packed trail
Best season: Year-round
Other trail users: Equestrians
Canine compatibility: Leashed dogs permitted

Land status: Operated by Missouri State Parks
Fees and permits: None
Maps: USGS Ware; trail maps available at visitor center
Trail contact: Trail of Tears State Park, 429 Moccasin Springs Rd., Jackson, MO 63755; (573) 334-1711; https://mostateparks.com/trails/trail-tears-state-park?type=hiking

Finding the trailhead: From St. Louis, take I-55 South for 102 miles to exit 105 toward Fruitland. Turn left (east) onto US 61 North / High Street and drive 1.1 miles to MO 177. Turn right (east) onto MO 177 and continue 7.4 miles to a stop sign. Turn right (south) to stay on MO 177 and drive 2.9 miles to the park entrance. Turn left (north) onto Hill Road and drive 0.4 mile to Overlook Road. Turn left (north) onto Overlook Road and drive 0.1 mile to the Pee-Wah Trail parking area on the left. **GPS:** N37 27.386' / W89 29.280'

The Hike

Trail of Tears State Park is a certified site on the Trail of Tears National Historic Trail. During the winter of 1838–39, more than 16,000 Cherokee were forced to leave their homelands in and around western North Carolina and take an 800-mile journey to Indian Territory in the west. Nearly one in four of the Cherokee who embarked on the journey died on the trail. Harsh weather, hunger, and disease all contributed to the deaths and the trail became known as the Trail of Tears. To learn more about the Trail of Tears National Historic Trail, visit the park's visitor center or www.nps.gov/trte.

Composed of two loops, the Pee-Wah Trail is the longest and most challenging trail in Trail of Tears State Park. Winding through the 1,300-acre Indian Creek Wild Area, be on the lookout for oak and hickory trees. Hikers will easily spot tulip poplars during the summer months. Also known as yellow poplars, these beautiful tall trees have large tulip-like flowers that are orange and green.

There are two trailheads for the Pee-Wah Trail. This guide lists directions from the "lower trailhead." The lower trailhead is located on the northwest end of the small gravel parking area and marked with a trail sign and information board.

Pee-Wah trailhead ▶

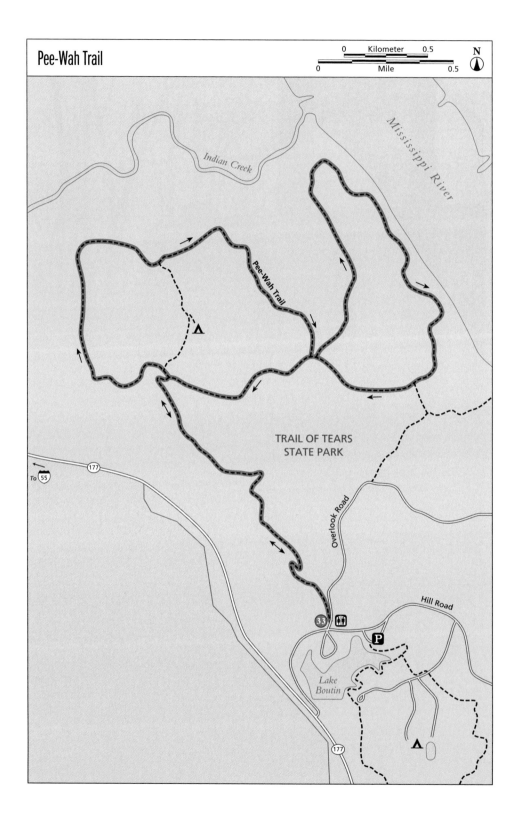

Pee-Wah Trail

0   Kilometer   0.5

0   Mile   0.5

N

Mississippi River

Indian Creek

Pee-Wah Trail

TRAIL OF TEARS
STATE PARK

To 55

177

Overlook Road

Hill Road

33

P

Lake
Boutin

177

Begin hiking northwest on the obvious dirt trail as it descends into a valley and crosses several small drainages. At 1.1 miles reach the floor of the valley and begin to climb the moderately steep ridge. At 1.6 miles reach the beginning of the loop portion of the hike and take the west (left) fork to hike the trail in a clockwise direction. After a short distance you will come to a spur trail, branching north, that leads to the backcountry camping area. Continue west and north for about 1 mile, at which point the trail bends to the east and crosses a rocky drainage. At 2.8 miles come to a connector trail, which branches south and leads to the backcountry camping area. Stay left (east) to continue on the Pee-Wah Trail.

At 3.7 miles come to the intersection of the two loops. Take the trail that branches to the northeast to continue hiking the full Pee-Wah Trail in a clockwise direction (the trail that bends back to the west will lead you to the beginning of the loop hike after 0.65 mile). Follow the trail as it leads generally north, descending into a valley and then climbing another ridge. At 4.5 miles you will be rewarded with your first good view of the Mississippi River. At this point the trail bends south and traverses the towering limestone bluffs that parallel the river.

At 5.3 miles come to a trail intersection. Stay right (southwest) to continue on the Pee-Wah Trail. At 5.8 miles come to another trail intersection. Stay right (west) to continue on the Pee-Wah Trail (the trail to the southeast leads to the upper trailhead). At 6.2 miles return to the intersection of the two loops. Stay left (southwest) to finish the loop portion of the hike. At 6.9 miles come to the end of the loop portion of the hike and turn south, hiking 1.6 miles back to the trailhead and parking area.

Miles and Directions

0.0 Begin hiking northwest on the obvious dirt path.

1.1 Reach the valley floor and climb a moderately steep ridge.

1.6 Come to the beginning of the loop portion of the hike and turn left (west).

2.6 The trail bends to the east and crosses a rocky drainage.

2.8 At the intersection with the connector trail, continue east to stay on the Pee-Wah Trail.

3.7 Come to the intersection of the two loops and stay left (northeast).

4.5 The trail takes a sharp turn to the south.

5.3 Come to a trail intersection and stay to the right (southwest).

5.8 Come to another trail intersection and stay to the right (west).

6.2 Return to the intersection of the two loops. Stay left (southwest) to finish the loop portion of the hike.

6.9 Reach the end of the loop portion of the hike. Turn south to return to the trailhead and parking area.

8.5 Arrive back at the trailhead and parking area.

34 Piney Creek Ravine Trail

Featuring the largest concentration of prehistoric rock art in Illinois, Piney Creek Ravine Trail offers visitors a pleasant day hike rich in both natural and cultural history.

Start: North from trailhead parking area
Distance: 2-mile lollipop
Hiking time: 1.5 hours
Difficulty: Moderate due to modest climb
Trail surface: Grass and dirt packed trail
Best season: Fall through spring
Other trail users: None

Canine compatibility: Leashed dogs permitted
Land status: Operated by Illinois Department of Natural Resources
Fees and permits: None
Map: USGS Welge
Trail contact: Piney Creek Ravine, 4301 S. Lake Dr., Chester, IL 62233; (618) 826-2706

Finding the trailhead: From St. Louis, take I-55 South to I-255 East, toward Illinois. Cross the Jefferson Barracks Bridge into Illinois and continue 5 miles to IL 3. Take IL 3 south through Columbia, Waterloo, Red Bud, Ruma, Ellis Grove, and Chester. South of Chester there is a large brown sign for Piney Creek Ravine directing you to turn left onto Hog Hill Road / CR 20. Follow Hog Hill for 3.8 miles to the intersection with Degognia Road. Turn right (east) and then immediately left (north), staying on CR 20, which is now Rock Crusher Road. Continue on CR 20 / Rock Crusher Road for 1.1 miles to Piney Creek Road. Turn left (west) onto Piney Creek Road and drive 1.6 miles to the large, gravel parking area on the right (east). **GPS: N37 53.426' / W89 38.292'**

The Hike

In 1972 the Illinois Department of Natural Resources purchased the 198-acre area known as Piney Creek Ravine. Now a State Natural Area and National Natural Landmark, Piney Creek Ravine is well known in the area for its rare plant species and its abundance of "rock art," which is believed to date back to the late Woodland (AD 500–1000) and Mississippian (AD 1000–1550) eras.

Piney Creek Ravine is one of only two places in Illinois that shortleaf pines grow naturally. The ravine forms a moist, sheltered habitat for mosses and liverworts to grow, but also offers dry, exposed bluffs perfect for post and blackjack oaks. Hikers coming to Piney Creek Ravine may encounter opossums, cottontails, chipmunks, whitetail deer, fence lizards, rough green snakes, and copperhead snakes. Timber rattlesnakes have never been reported but are a possibility in the area.

Piney Creek Ravine Trail is a 2-mile lollipop hike that begins in a field, of all places. Hikers will quickly find themselves entering the ravine after a short walk through the field. Many visitors find that the 2 miles take longer than anticipated after finding and exploring the area's numerous petroglyphs and pictographs. You will also

Top: Piney Creek
Bottom: Rock art at Piney Creek ▶

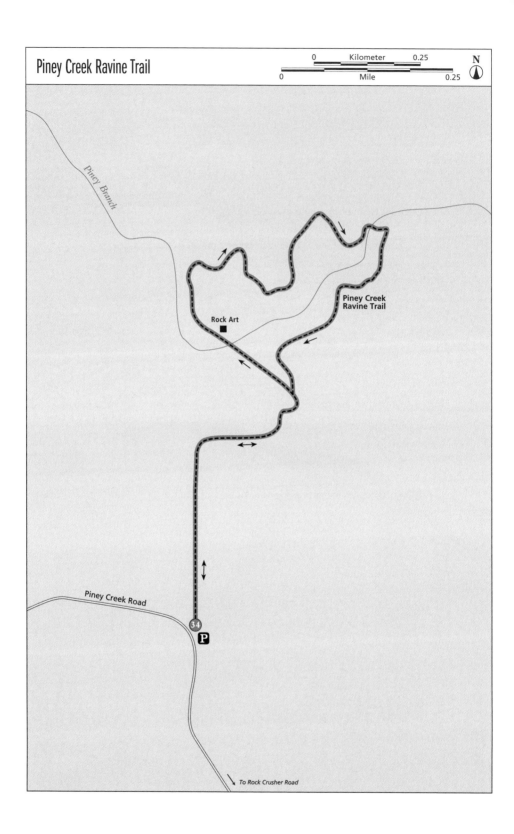

Piney Creek Ravine Trail

0   Kilometer   0.25

0   Mile   0.25

N

Piney Branch

Piney Creek
Ravine Trail

Rock Art

Piney Creek Road

34

P

To Rock Crusher Road

find an abundance of graffiti in this area, some of which dates back to early settlers and some much more recent.

From the small parking area, locate the information kiosk and begin hiking north on an access lane. Following the fence line, continue on this grassy path until you reach an interpretive sign at 0.3 mile. At this point follow the dirt trail, which is marked with a hiker symbol and an arrow, east down a small hill and into a grove of cedar trees. At 0.5 mile, where the trail forks, stay left and follow the sign, which points the way to the rock art. Shortly after, the trail turns to the left (west) and crosses the shallow creek. Carefully look for the trail on the other side of the creek and continue west. Immediately come to another fork in the trail at 0.6 mile. Follow the spur trail to the right to view the rock art.

After exploring the petroglyphs and pictographs, return to the main trail and hike west. At 1.0 mile follow the trail as it descends through shortleaf pines to a creek. Cross the creek and continue, coming to the beginning of the loop at 1.5 miles. Return to the parking area via the same route.

Miles and Directions

0.0   Begin hiking north along the grassy access lane.

0.3   Reach the interpretive sign and follow the trail east.

0.5   Stay left (northwest) at the fork in the trail and shortly after turn left (west), crossing the shallow creek.

0.6   Take the spur trail to the right (east) to view the rock art, then return to the main trail to continue the hike.

1.0   The trail descends through shortleaf pine trees.

1.1   Cross the creek.

1.5   Return to the beginning of the loop and follow the same route to the south that you hiked in on.

2.0   Arrive back at the trailhead.

GREEN TIP

Be extra careful to preserve our natural and cultural historical areas, including their petroglyphs, pictographs, and artifacts, so that future generations can learn from them too.

35 Waterfall Trail

Featuring a series of small, wet-weather waterfalls, this moderate day hike is a great choice in the Shawnee National Forest.

Start: South end of Hidden Cove Trailhead parking area
Distance: 6.4 miles out and back
Hiking time: 3 to 4 hours
Difficulty: Difficult due to length and several modestly steep inclines
Trail surface: Dirt packed trail
Best season: Spring and fall
Other trail users: Equestrians

Canine compatibility: Leashed dogs permitted
Land status: Operated by Shawnee National Forest
Fees and permits: None
Map: USGS Kincaid
Trail contact: Shawnee National Forest, 50 Highway 145 South, Harrisburg, IL 62946; (618) 253-7114; www.fs.usda.gov/recarea/shawnee/recarea/?recid=28020

Finding the trailhead: From St. Louis, take I-64 East across the Mississippi River into Illinois. Merge right onto IL 3 South after crossing the bridge. Drive 80.2 miles on IL 3 South through the cities/towns of Columbia, Waterloo, Red Bud, and Chester before turning left onto IL 151. Drive 1 mile to Gum Ridge Road and turn right (east) onto Gum Ridge Road. Continue 2.1 miles and turn right (south) onto John Lee Road. Follow John Lee Road until it ends at the Hidden Cove Trailhead parking area. **GPS:** N37 49.021'/W89 29.926'

The Hike

The Shawnee National Forest is an incredibly diverse area, rich in both natural and cultural history. Home to hundreds of species of wildlife, the Shawnee National Forest is a true treasure in southern Illinois. Several species of threatened and endangered species can be found in the forest, including the eastern small-footed bat, the bald eagle, and the bird-voiced tree frog.

Located near Kincaid Lake, the Waterfall Trail showcases many highlights of the Shawnee National Forest. The main attractions of this trail are a series of small, wet-weather waterfalls and the interesting limestone and sandstone formations. It is possible to do this hike as a shuttle, but it is described as an out-and-back hike here.

From the south end of the Hidden Cove Trailhead parking area, locate the trailhead for the Waterfall Trail. You will see an old, rickety bridge, which used to be the beginning of the trail. Instead of crossing this bridge, turn east and follow the new trail (marked by white diamonds). Rock-hop across the creek and continue following the diamond-marked trail east.

At 0.2 mile come to the top of a small hill and catch a glimpse of Kincaid Lake. The trail makes a sharp turn to the west, heading away from the lake. At 0.9 mile cross a small drainage and climb a short but moderately steep ridge. At 1.0 mile you will see a small pond to the north.

Fungi on Waterfall Trail

At 1.6 miles you'll come to a small creek. Follow the creek east and you will see the first of a series of small waterfalls. Like most waterfalls in the Shawnee National Forest, this series of waterfalls relies on recent rainfall in the area. This is a great place to take a break, have a picnic, or just enjoy the scenery. After exploring the falls, continue on the Waterfall Trail as it wanders through the hardwood forest. Crossing several small ridges and valleys, it is easy to get lost in the subtle beauty of this area.

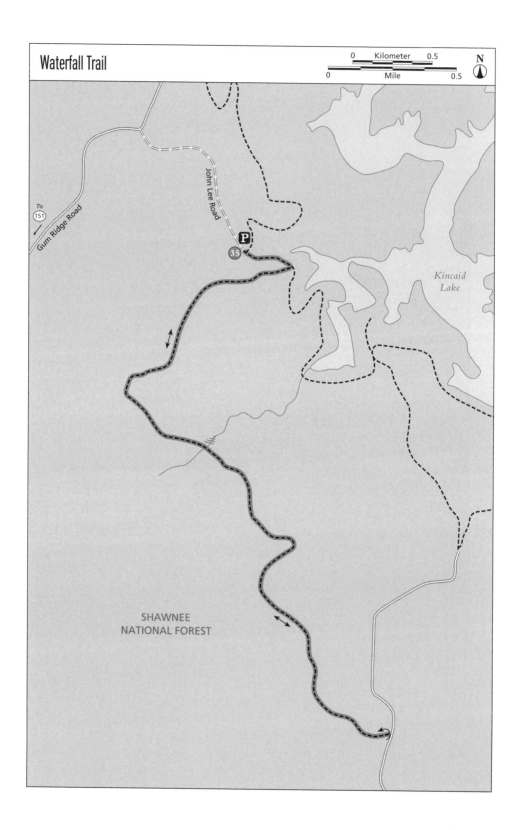

Waterfall Trail

Kilometer
Mile

N

To 151

Gum Ridge Road

John Lee Road

P
35

Kincaid
Lake

SHAWNEE
NATIONAL FOREST

At 2.6 miles cross a series of small, rocky drainages and begin to ascend a final steep ridge to the southern end of the Waterfall Trail. At 3.2 miles you will find another small parking area, a yellow gate blocking motor vehicles from entering the trail, and a wooden sign pointing hikers and equestrians to the Hidden Cove Trailhead and Waterfall Trail. If you have not set up a shuttle, turn around here and return to the trailhead via the same route.

Miles and Directions

0.0 Follow the diamond-marked trail southeast, crossing a small creek.

0.2 Come to the top of a small hill, where the trail takes a sharp turn to the west.

0.9 Cross a small drainage and climb a short, steep ridge.

1.0 Pass a small pond to the north of the trail.

1.6 Come to a small creek and waterfall area.

2.6 Cross a series of small, rocky drainages.

3.2 Arrive at the southern end of the trail. If you have not arranged a shuttle, turn around and return to the trailhead via the same route.

6.4 Arrive back at the trailhead.

GREEN TIP

When using iodine to purify your drinking water, be sure to add the iodine to your water away from the original water source. Even the smallest drop of iodine can hurt and even kill numerous plants, bugs, or animals that depend on the water.

36 Pomona Natural Bridge

The Pomona Natural Bridge hike is one of the many hidden treasures within the rolling hills of southern Illinois. Located about 30 minutes from Carbondale, Illinois, the area offers a beautiful retreat for anybody, especially families seeking a place to picnic and enjoy a short hike. Of course, the natural stone bridge is the highlight of the area.

Start: West of parking area
Distance: 0.5-mile lollipop
Hiking time: 0.5 hour
Difficulty: Easy due to short distance
Trail surface: Gravel, rock, and dirt packed trail
Best season: Year-round
Other trail users: None
Canine compatibility: Leashed dogs permitted

Land status: Operated by Shawnee National Forest
Fees and permits: None
Map: USGS Pomona
Trail contact: Shawnee National Forest, 50 Highway 145 South, Harrisburg, IL 62946; (618) 253-7114; www.fs.usda.gov/recarea/ shawnee/recarea/?recid=10678

Finding the trailhead: From St. Louis, take I-64 East across the Mississippi River into Illinois. Merge right onto IL 3 after crossing the bridge. Drive 80.2 miles on IL 3 South through the cities/ towns of Columbia, Waterloo, Red Bud, and Chester before turning left onto IL 149 East toward Murphysboro. Continue 8.1 miles into and through the city of Murphysboro. On the east side of the city, turn right onto IL 127 South. Continue on IL 127 South for 8.9 miles before turning right onto Pomona Road. Drive 0.8 mile into the small town of Pomona and turn right onto Sadler Road at the three-way stop. Stay on Sadler for only 0.1 mile before turning right onto Natural Bridge Road. Follow Natural Bridge Road for 2.1 miles until it dead-ends in the parking area. **GPS:** N37 38.916'/W89 20.582'

The Hike

The Pomona Natural Bridge lies in the Shawnee National Forest and provides an ideal area for families to enjoy a natural playground that includes trail hiking, a natural bridge, and even a hidden cave. The sandstone bridge is 90 feet long and is as wide as 8 feet in some places. The bridge has slowly been carved out over the years and is anywhere from 20 to 30 feet off the ground. A small creek trickles below the bridge for most of the year but becomes much larger during the rainy seasons, when it attempts to continue wearing away the soft sandstone.

In the large parking area (we have seen two or three buses here before), hikers can locate restrooms just south of the trailhead as well as several picnic tables in the area. Locate the gravel trail to the west of the parking area and begin an immediate downhill hike. The trail is well maintained and even has a fence/handrail along the steeper portion.

Pomona Natural Bridge

Fall in southern Illinois

After 0.1 mile hikers will find themselves in typical southern Illinois hardwood woodland as they reach the loop portion of the hike. Cherry, black walnut, and tulip trees are just a few of the species to be enjoyed by tree lovers. Stay left (southwest) and continue hiking for another 0.2 mile before reaching the Pomona Natural Bridge. A few benches can be found along the trail for nature lovers to sit and enjoy while explorers check out the bridge and even drop down into the ravine to look for a hidden cave and/or other natural wonders.

Continue hiking east across the bridge after enjoying some time here. After crossing the bridge, the trail climbs slightly for 0.1 mile before reaching the end of the loop. Return to the parking lot by hiking uphill for the last 0.1 mile.

SOUTHERN ILLINOIS WINE COUNTRY

Did you know that the Pomona Natural Bridge sits in the heart of southern Illinois's wine country? The Wine Trail (www.shawneewinetrail.com) connects many of the wineries and is a popular way to spend the day.

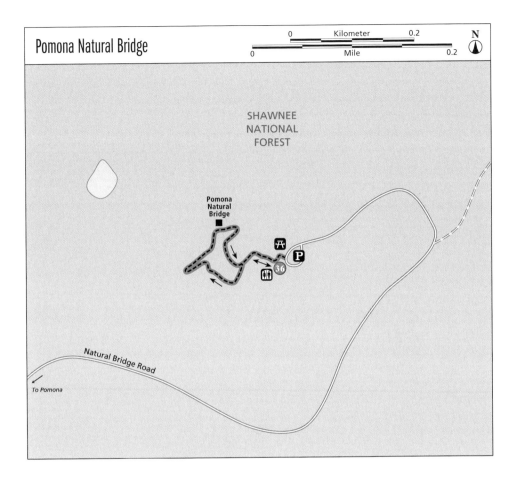

Pomona Natural Bridge

SHAWNEE
NATIONAL
FOREST

Pomona
Natural
Bridge

36 P

Natural Bridge Road

To Pomona

Miles and Directions

0.0 Begin hiking west as the gravel trail descends from the parking area.

0.1 Stay left where the loop section of the hike begins.

0.3 Reach the Pomona Natural Bridge and cross the bridge.

0.4 Stay left where the loop section of the hike ends.

0.5 Arrive back at the parking area.

37 Little Grand Canyon Trail

This loop hike in the Shawnee National Forest features exposed bluffs, an erosion-carved canyon, a seasonal waterfall, and several rock overhangs, making it one of the most interesting areas in the entire region. The parking area offers several picnic sites and an outhouse for visitors looking to enjoy a longer stay.

Start: Southwest corner of trailhead parking area

Distance: 3-mile loop

Hiking time: 2 hours

Difficulty: Difficult due to steep climbs and slippery rocks

Trail surface: Dirt packed trail and rock

Best season: Fall through spring

Other trail users: None

Canine compatibility: Leashed dogs permitted

Land status: Operated by Shawnee National Forest

Fees and permits: None

Map: USGS Gorham

Trail contact: Shawnee National Forest, 50 Highway 145 South, Harrisburg, IL 62946; (618) 253-7114; www.fs.usda.gov/recarea/shawnee/recarea/?recid=27713

Finding the trailhead: From St. Louis, take I-64 East for 1 mile, crossing over into Illinois. Merge onto IL 3 South toward Cahokia and follow IL 3 for 84.2 miles through the towns of Columbia, Waterloo, and Chester. Continue 25 miles on IL 3 from Chester before turning left onto Town Creek Road, then travel 6.6 miles to Hickory Ridge Road. Turn right onto Hickory Ridge Road and continue 4 miles to a four-way stop; turn right to stay on Hickory Ridge Road. Drive 2.3 miles and turn right onto Little Grand Canyon Road. Follow Little Grand Canyon Road until it dead-ends in the parking area. The trailhead is located at the southwest corner of the parking area. **GPS:** N37 40.842' / W89 23.719'

The Hike

The Little Grand Canyon National Natural Landmark is a small but dramatic part of the 280,000-acre Shawnee National Forest. Located in Jackson County, Illinois, the deep box canyon has been slowly eroding over time and now boasts exposed, majestic bluffs.

Visitors to the Little Grand Canyon area will witness typical southern Illinois landscapes. Rich oak and hickory forests tower above sycamore and beech trees. Just south of the Little Grand Canyon is a place known as Snake Road. Each year the road is closed to accommodate several species of snakes, including timber rattlesnakes, western cottonmouths, and the endangered green water snake, as they migrate to and from their winter hibernation spots, which include the Little Grand Canyon.

The Little Grand Canyon Trail is a 3-mile hike that begins with a roller-coaster-like ridge ascent to a scenic overlook. Hikers can stop, enjoy the view, and return to the parking lot, or continue into the canyon below.

Little Grand Canyon passage to trailhead ▶

Little Grand Canyon Trail

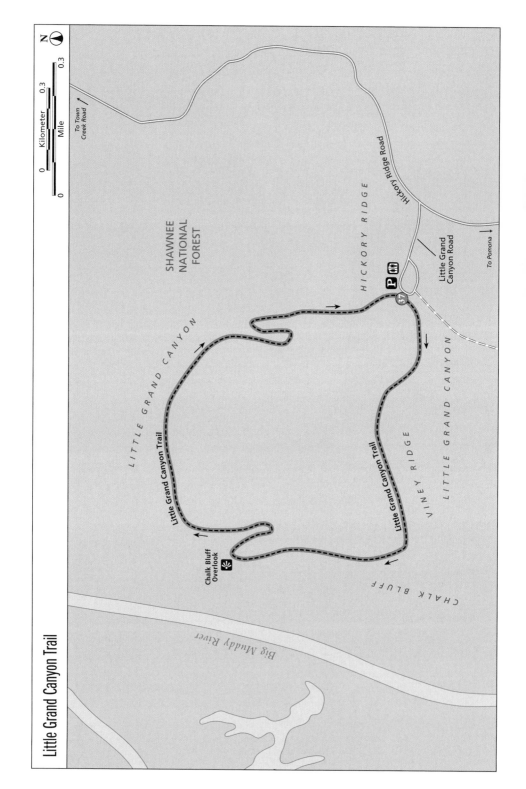

Moss-covered drainage on the Little Grand Canyon Trail

The trailhead is located at the southwest corner of the parking area, just to the right (west) of the outhouses. Begin hiking southwest on the obvious gravel and dirt trail. Follow the trail as it traverses Viney Ridge through a thick forest of maple, oak, sassafras, beech, and tulip trees. Pass several wooden benches before reaching a large scenic overlook on Chalk Bluff at 1.2 miles. Here you have a good view of the Big Muddy River to the west. At this point the trail curves to the right (southeast) and begins to gradually descend the ridge.

At 1.4 miles the trail grows noticeable steeper and you enter the moss-covered sandstone canyon. Carefully descend, alternating between following the trail and the natural drainage. Look closely and you will notice that steps have been etched into the rock in several areas, a work project completed by the Civilian Conservation Corps in the 1930s.

At 1.8 miles reach the bottom of the canyon and begin following the trail, now marked with white diamonds, to the east. Cross a small creek at 2.1 miles and continue east, passing tall bluffs. At 2.4 miles the trail curves to the right (south) and into another slippery sandstone drainage. Follow the drainage, again using caution and looking for steps as you pass over several small, seasonal waterfalls. At the top of the drainage, turn left (east) and ascend the moderately steep trail back to the parking area.

Miles and Directions

0.0 Begin hiking southwest along Viney Ridge.

1.2 Come to the scenic overlook at Chalk Bluff.

1.4 Descend the slippery sandstone canyon.

1.8 Reach the bottom of the canyon and begin hiking east.

2.1 Cross a small creek and continue hiking east.

2.4 Come to the second sandstone canyon and carefully ascend, hiking south. At the top of the canyon, turn left (east) onto the obvious dirt trail.

3.0 Arrive back at the parking area.

A FEW NOTES ON ALTO PASS

The village of Alto Pass, Illinois, was founded by travelers who continuously found themselves and their wagons stuck in one of the Shawnee's numerous springs. While traveling from Anna to Carbondale, travelers finally settled Alto Pass as a halfway point to rest after a long day of getting wagons unstuck. Oddly enough, today Alto Pass tends to be a large mudding and 4x4 draw in the southern Illinois area.

Alto Pass is also the gateway to Bald Knob Cross. Visitors to the area will likely notice the giant cross that has been built on top of one of the higher points in southern Illinois. Even travelers in Missouri can see the cross from miles away.

38 Trillium Trail

Giant City State Park offers some of the finest scenery in southern Illinois. Located in the Shawnee National Forest, the park features two different bluffs for rock climbers, horseback riding and stables, picnicking, and short scenic hikes like the Trillium Trail. The Trillium offers views of the Fern Rocks Nature Preserve.

Start: South of trailhead parking area
Distance: 1.25-mile loop
Hiking time: 1 hour
Difficulty: Moderate due to rugged trail
Trail surface: Dirt packed trail and rock
Best season: Year-round
Other trail users: None
Canine compatibility: Leashed dogs permitted

Land status: Operated by Illinois Department of Natural Resources
Fees and permits: None
Maps: USGS Makanda; park map available at visitor center
Trail contact: Giant City State Park, 235 Giant City Rd., Makanda, IL 62958; (618) 457-4836; www.dnr.illinois.gov/parks/pages/giantcity.aspx

Finding the trailhead: From St. Louis, take I-64 East for 78 miles to I-57 South. Drive on I-57 South for 38.5 miles toward Carbondale to IL 13 West at exit 54B. Drive 15 miles into the city of Carbondale and turn left onto Giant City Road. Continue on Giant City Road for 10.7 miles (pass the visitor center on the right at 10.2 miles) and turn right onto Giant City Lodge Road. Drive 0.5 mile and turn right onto Stone Fort Road. Continue 2.1 miles on Stone Fort Road to the Trillium Trail parking area on the left. **GPS:** N37 37.494'/W89 12.218'

The Hike

Rich in both natural and cultural history, southern Illinois offers many options for outdoor enthusiasts. One of the highlights of the area is the 4,000-acre Giant City State Park, located just south of Carbondale, near the small artist community of Makanda. The park boasts nearly 1.2 million visitors a year and is surrounded by the Shawnee National Forest. Hikers, horseback riders, rock climbers, campers, birders, geologists, history buffs, and nature lovers come to the park in search of outdoor recreation and solitude. Evidence of early human habitation in the area dates back 10,000 years and can be found in several of the shelter bluffs in the park. The park provides a little something for everyone.

One of the more rugged trails in the park, the Trillium Trail is a must-do for nature lovers. If you choose to hike this 1.25-mile loop trail, you will experience many of the park's best features, including towering 70-foot bluffs and an incredibly diverse forest ecosystem. The park is home to more than seventy-five species of trees and hundreds of species of wildflowers. Keep an eye out for the trail's namesake flowering plant, the trillium. This plant is easily identified by its white or pink blooms.

Sandstone bluffs along Trillium Trail

Locate the trailhead just south of the parking area and marked with a sign, which indicates the beginning of the trail. Begin hiking east as the trail parallels Stone Fort Road for a short distance. At about 0.5 mile the trail bears to the right (south) and begins to ascend a steep bluff via a series of stairs. Reach the top of the bluff at 0.6 mile and follow the trail north and then east along the ridge. At 0.9 mile, just before the trail begins to descend the ridge, you will have good views of the impressive

VULTURE FEST

If you decide to visit Giant City State Park in the fall, keep an eye to the sky, as you may witness the annual turkey vulture migration through the area. The giant scavengers, which make their nests in the tall trees and bluffs in the area, are celebrated each October in nearby Makanda, Illinois. Vulture Fest is a unique event put on by the small artist community and offers food, crafts, and entertainment. Visit the city's website (http://villageofmakanda .com/events.html) for more information.

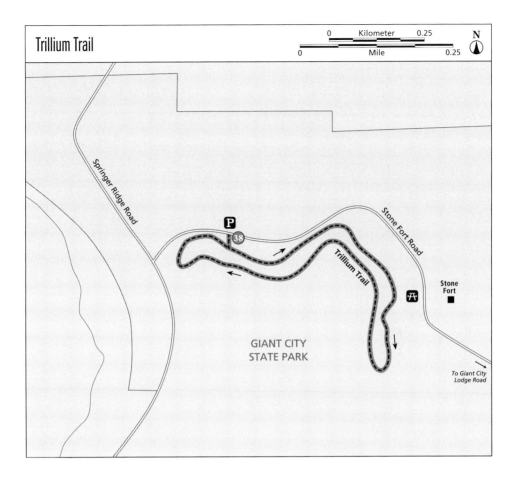

Trillium Trail

0 Kilometer 0.25
0 Mile 0.25

N

Springer Ridge Road

Stone Fort Road

P 38

Trillium Trail

Stone Fort

GIANT CITY STATE PARK

To Giant City Lodge Road

Makanda Bluff to the north. At 1.25 miles reach the end of the loop and the trailhead parking area.

Miles and Directions

0.0 Begin hiking east from the Trillium Trail parking area and trailhead.

0.5 The trail begins to ascend a steep bluff.

0.6 Turn right (north) at the top of the bluff and follow the trail.

0.9 Enjoy views of Makanda Bluff to the north.

1.25 Arrive back at the trailhead.

39 Giant City Nature Trail

The Giant City Nature Trail is a favorite for regular visitors to Giant City State Park. Located near the Devil's Standtable, an amazing rock formation, the nature trail is perfect for wildlife viewing, photography, and exploring. Nearby picnic areas make for a full day of outdoor recreation.

Start: South from parking area
Distance: 1.1-mile lollipop
Hiking time: 1.5 hours
Difficulty: Easy due to flat terrain
Trail surface: Dirt packed trail, gravel, and rock
Best season: Year-round
Other trail users: None
Canine compatibility: Leashed dogs permitted

Land status: Operated by Illinois Department of Natural Resources
Fees and permits: None
Maps: USGS Makanda; park map available at visitor center
Trail contact: Giant City State Park, 235 Giant City Rd., Makanda, IL 62958; (618) 457-4836; www.dnr.illinois.gov/parks/pages/giantcity.aspx

Finding the trailhead: From St. Louis, take I-64 East for 78 miles to I-57 South. Drive on I-57 South for 38.5 miles toward Carbondale to IL 13 West at exit 54B. Drive 15 miles into the city of Carbondale and turn left onto Giant City Road. Continue on Giant City Road for 10.7 miles and turn right onto Giant City Lodge Road. Drive 0.5 mile and turn left onto Stone Fort Road. Continue 0.4 mile on Stone Fort Road to the Shelter #2 parking area on the right. **GPS:** N37 35.874'/W89 11.510'

The Hike

This short nature trail is beautiful year-round. In the spring hundreds of species of wildflowers grow on and around the massive sandstone structures; in the summer the towering tree canopy provides hikers and wildlife with a respite from the sun; in the fall hikers are treated to a wash of fall color from more than seventy-five species of trees; and in the winter icicles hang delicately from the overhanging cliffs.

Southern Illinois is rich in both natural and cultural history, and Giant City State Park offers visitors many opportunities to explore them. Hikers and horseback riders will enjoy more than 17 miles of trails. Rock climbers of all ability levels can choose from two different cliff faces that have been designated for climbing and rappelling. Picnic areas, playgrounds, an interpretive visitor center, and the historic Giant City Lodge round out the options offered at this park.

One of the most popular trails in the park is the Giant City Nature Trail. This 1.1-mile trail showcases some of the things that make the park so special, including the Giant City Streets, huge sandstone bluffs that jut up on both sides of the trail.

The sandstone bluffs known as the "Giant City Streets" ▶

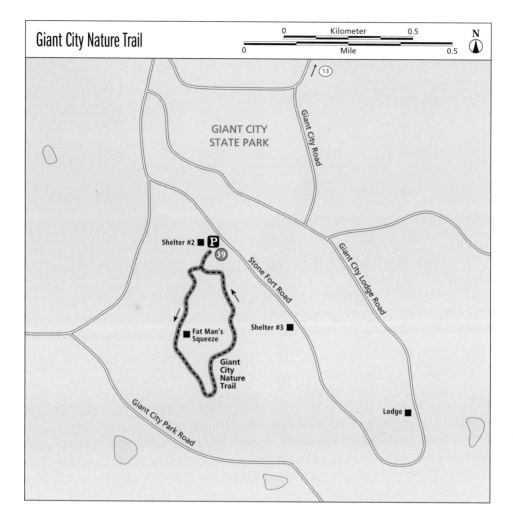

Giant City Nature Trail

From the Shelter #2 parking area, locate the unmarked trail to the south and hike south on the obvious dirt path for 0.1 mile. At 0.1 mile come to the main loop trail and turn right (west). At 0.2 mile you'll arrive at a boardwalk that goes across rough terrain and leads you to the beginning of the Giant City Streets.

At 0.3 mile come to an unmarked feature known as Fat Man's Squeeze. This narrow crack leads the adventurous and thin through the sandstone bluff, although caution should be used when deciding just how daring you want to be. In the past Fat Man's Squeeze has been closed due to nesting copperhead snakes. The narrow passage has also trapped several hikers, as it can be very difficult to dislodge one's self from the grippy limestone walls. Closures should be taken seriously.

At Fat Man's Squeeze the trail makes an abrupt right-hand turn. Follow the trail as it leads through more interesting rock formations.

At 0.6 mile the trail heads north up a moderately steep hill. At the top of the hill, you can take a break and catch your breath before heading down the other side of the ridge. At 0.8 mile come to the spur trail that leads to Shelter #3. Stay to the left (west) to continue on the trail. At 1.0 mile return to the spur trail that leads to Shelter #2; turn right and follow this spur trail north to the parking area.

Miles and Directions

0.0 From the Shelter #2 parking area, begin hiking south onto the unmarked Giant City Nature Trail.

0.1 The unmarked trail joins the main loop. Continue right (southwest).

0.2 The trail becomes a boardwalk.

0.3 Reach Fat Man's Squeeze and turn right (west) and then left (south) to stay on the nature trail.

0.6 Climb a moderately steep hill.

0.8 Pass the trail on the right that goes to Shelter #3 and continue west.

1.0 Reach the spur trail that leads back to Shelter #2. Turn right (north).

1.1 Arrive back at the trailhead and parking area.

NEARBY TRAILS

There are six additional trails in Giant City State Park. The Arrowwood Self-Interpretive Nature Trail is a 0.3-mile trail that educates park visitors on some of the many tree species found in the park. The Devil's Standtable Nature Trail is a 0.3-mile trail that focuses on one of the park's most unusual geographic features, an amazing rock formation. The 0.3-mile Stone Fort Nature Trail explores the area's cultural history, and the Post Oak Nature Trail is a 0.3-mile wheelchair-accessible nature trail that features a small pond and several overlooks. The Indian Creek Nature Trail is a 0.8-mile loop trail through a mature floodplain forest. And those looking for an overnight trip should check out the 12-mile Red Cedar Hiking Trail.

40 Panther Den Trail

A short stroll in the Shawnee National Forest, the Panther Den Trail provides easy access to one of the most interesting rock formations in the area. A short hike allows for hours of exploration.

Start: Northeast from trailhead parking area
Distance: 2.8 miles out and back
Hiking time: 2 hours
Difficulty: Moderate
Trail surface: Dirt packed trail
Best season: Fall through spring
Other trail users: Equestrians
Canine compatibility: Leashed dogs permitted

Land status: Operated by Shawnee National Forest
Fees and permits: None
Map: USGS Lick Creek
Trail contact: Shawnee National Forest, 50 Highway 145 South, Harrisburg, IL 62946; (618) 253-7114; www.fs.usda.gov/recarea/shawnee/recarea/?recid=34603

Finding the trailhead: From St. Louis, take I-64 East for 78 miles to I-57 South. Drive on I-57 South for 38.5 miles toward Carbondale to IL 13 West at exit 54B. Drive 15 miles into the city of Carbondale and turn left onto Giant City Road. Continue on Giant City Road for 7 miles to Grassy Road. Turn left onto Grassy Road and drive 3 miles before turning right onto Rocky Comfort Road. Follow Rocky Comfort Road (staying right at 1.9 miles at the Y) for 4.1 miles to Panthers Den Road. Turn left and drive 1.5 miles to Panthers Den Lane. Turn left again and drive 0.6 mile down the gravel road to the parking area and trailhead on the right. **GPS:** N37 34.782' / W89 5.295'

The Hike

In 1990 the US Congress designated southern Illinois's Panther Den as a wilderness area. Of the Panther Den Wilderness Area's 1,195 acres, the Shawnee National Forest manages 1,081 acres and the Crab Orchard National Wildlife Refuge manages the remaining acreage.

The 160-mile River-to-River Trail runs through the Panther Den Wilderness Area and is the trail that receives the most recognition. However, the several trails that support and branch off of the River-to-River Trail offer some amazing opportunities. Hikers choosing the Panther Den Trail are in for a treat, as they will soon come into an area once believed to have been a large waterway that over time has created a hikers' playground. The Panther Den Trail is a quick, 2.8-mile, out-and-back hike that leaves plenty of time to explore a remarkable maze of 70-foot-high cliffs in which huge blocks have split off from one another to create a network of crevices, passageways, and cave-like "rooms."

From the parking area, locate the information kiosk and trailhead. Begin hiking northeast on the obvious dirt trail, Forest Service Trail 371. The Forest Service made

Maze of giant sandstone bluffs at Panther Den ▶

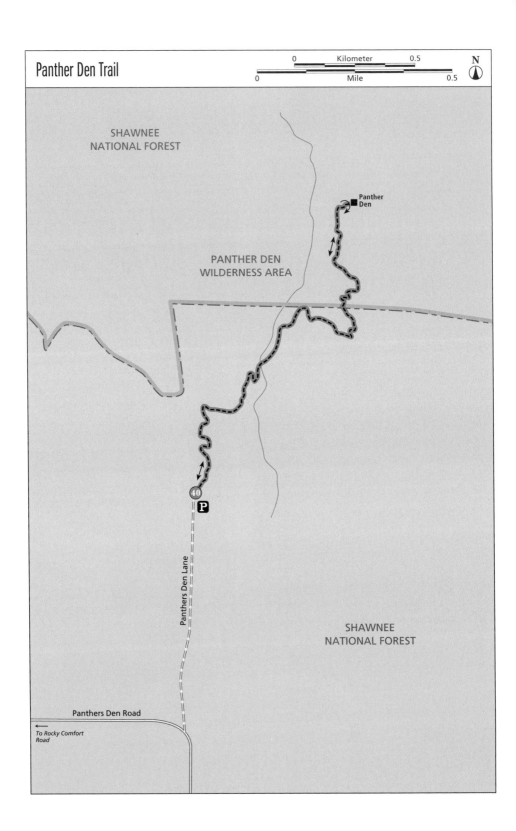

Panther Den Trail

0   Kilometer   0.5

0   Mile   0.5

N

SHAWNEE
NATIONAL FOREST

PANTHER DEN
WILDERNESS AREA

Panther
Den

40

P

Panthers Den Lane

SHAWNEE
NATIONAL FOREST

Panthers Den Road

To Rocky Comfort
Road

some much-needed improvements to this trail just a few years back as the area continued to grow in popularity.

At 0.4 mile cross the creek and continue hiking northeast. At 0.9 mile Forest Service Trail 371 joins the River-to-River Trail; stay left (north) onto the River-to-River Trail / Trail 371 and cross into the Panther Den Wilderness Area at 1.0 mile. Just after entering the wilderness area, the trail descends downhill for a short period before reaching the first view of some of the unique, towering rock walls of the Panther Den. Continue hiking north along the trail as the walls continue to get more and more prominent on your right (east).

After 1.4 mile reach the Panther Den and explore one of the many spur paths that lead through the labyrinth of rocks and cliffs. When you are through exploring, return to the trailhead via the same route.

Miles and Directions

0.0 From the trailhead, hike northeast on the obvious dirt trail.

0.4 Cross a creek and continue hiking northeast.

0.9 Forest Service Trail 371 joins the River-to-River Trail.

1.0 Reach the Panther Den Wilderness Area.

1.4 Arrive at the Panther Den.

2.8 Arrive back at the trailhead and parking area.

GREEN TIP
Before building a campfire, consider the conditions around you. First, are campfires permitted? If so, is there an established fire ring to use? We recommend wood that is dead, down, dry, and dinky.

Panther Den Trail

The Art of Hiking

When standing nose to nose with a mountain lion, you're probably not too concerned with the issue of ethical behavior in the wild. No doubt you're just terrified. But let's be honest. How often are you nose to nose with a mountain lion? For most of us, a hike into the "wild" means loading up the SUV with expensive gear and driving to a toileted trailhead. Sure, you can mourn how civilized we've become—how GPS units have replaced natural instinct and Gore-Tex stands in for true-grit—but the silly gadgets of civilization aside, we have plenty of reason to take pride in how we've matured. With survival now on the back burner, we've begun to understand that we have a responsibility to protect, no longer just conquer, our wild places: that they, not we, are at risk. So please, do what you can. The following section will help you understand better what it means to "do what you can" while still making the most of your hiking experience. Anyone can take a hike, but hiking safely and well is an art requiring preparation and proper equipment.

Trail Etiquette

Leave No Trace. Always leave an area just like you found it—if not better than you found it. Avoid camping in fragile, alpine meadows and along the banks of streams and lakes. Use a camp stove versus building a wood fire. Pack up all of your trash and extra food. Bury human waste at least 100 feet from water sources under 6 to 8 inches of topsoil. Don't bathe with soap in a lake, stream, or river—use prepackaged moistened towels to wipe off sweat and dirt, or bathe in the water without soap.

Stay on the trail. It's true, a path anywhere leads nowhere new, but purists will just have to get over it. Paths serve an important purpose; they limit impact on natural areas. Straying from a designated trail may seem innocent but it can cause damage to sensitive areas—damage that may take years to recover, if it can recover at all. Even simple shortcuts can be destructive. So, please, stay on the trail.

Leave no weeds. Noxious weeds tend to overtake other plants, which in turn affects animals and birds that depend on them for food. To minimize the spread of noxious weeds, hikers should regularly clean their boots, tents, packs, and hiking poles of mud and seeds. Also brush your dog to remove any weed seeds before heading off into a new area.

Keep your dog under control. You can buy a flexi-lead that allows your dog to go exploring along the trail, while allowing you the ability to reel him in should another hiker approach or should he decide to chase a rabbit. Always obey leash laws and be sure to bury your dog's waste or pack it in resealable plastic bags.

Respect other trail users. Often you're not the only one on the trail. With the rise in popularity of multiuse trails, you'll have to learn a new kind of respect, beyond the nod and "hello" approach you may be used to. First investigate whether you're on a multiuse trail, and assume the appropriate precautions. When you encounter motorized vehicles (ATVs, motorcycles, and 4WDs), be alert. Though they should always yield to the hiker, often they're going too fast or are too lost in the buzz of their engine to react to your presence. If you hear activity ahead, step off the trail just to be safe. Note that you're not likely to hear a mountain biker coming, so be prepared and know ahead of time whether you share the trail with them. Cyclists should always yield to hikers, but that's little comfort to the hiker. Be aware. When you approach horses or pack animals on the trail, always step quietly off the trail, preferably on the downhill side, and let them pass. If you're wearing a large backpack, it's often a good idea to sit down. To some animals, a hiker wearing a large backpack might appear threatening. Many national forests allow domesticated grazing, usually for sheep and cattle. Make sure your dog doesn't harass these animals, and respect ranchers' rights while you're enjoying yours.

Getting into Shape

Unless you want to be sore—and possibly have to shorten your trip or vacation—be sure to get in shape before a big hike. If you're terribly out of shape, start a walking program early, preferably eight weeks in advance. Start with a 15-minute walk during your lunch hour or after work and gradually increase your walking time to an hour. You should also increase your elevation gain. Walking briskly up hills really strengthens your leg muscles and gets your heart rate up. If you work in a storied office building, take the stairs instead of the elevator. If you prefer going to a gym, walk the treadmill or use a stair machine. You can further increase your strength and endurance by walking with a loaded backpack. Stationary exercises you might consider are squats, leg lifts, sit-ups, and push-ups. Other good ways to get in shape include biking, running, aerobics, and, of course, short hikes. Stretching before and after a hike keeps muscles flexible and helps avoid injuries.

Preparedness

It's been said that failing to plan means planning to fail. So do take the necessary time to plan your trip. Whether going on a short day hike or an extended backpack trip, always prepare for the worst. Simply remembering to pack a copy of the *US Army Survival Manual* is not preparedness. Although it's not a bad idea if you plan on entering truly wild places, it's merely the tourniquet answer to a problem. You need to do your best to prevent the problem from arising in the first place. In order to survive— and to stay reasonably comfortable—you need to concern yourself with the basics: water, food, and shelter. Don't go on a hike without having these bases covered. And don't go on a hike expecting to find these items in the woods.

Water. Even in frigid conditions, you need at least 2 quarts of water a day to function efficiently. Add heat and taxing terrain and you can bump that figure up to 1 gallon. That's simply a base to work from—your metabolism and your level of conditioning can raise or lower that amount. Unless you know your level, assume that you need 1 gallon of water a day. Now, where do you plan on getting the water?

Preferably not from natural water sources. These sources can be loaded with intestinal disturbers, such as bacteria, viruses, and fertilizers. *Giardia lamblia*, the most common of these disturbers, is a protozoan parasite that lives part of its life cycle as a cyst in water sources. The parasite spreads when mammals defecate in water sources. Once ingested, giardia can induce cramping, diarrhea, vomiting, and fatigue within two days to two weeks after ingestion. Giardiasis is treatable with prescription drugs. If you believe you've contracted giardiasis, see a doctor immediately.

Treating water. The best and easiest solution to avoid polluted water is to carry your water with you. Yet, depending on the nature of your hike and the duration, this may not be an option—1 gallon of water weighs 8½ pounds. In that case you'll need to look into treating water. Regardless of which method you choose, you should always carry some water with you in case of an emergency. Save this reserve until you absolutely need it.

There are three methods of treating water: boiling, chemical treatment, and filtering. If you boil water, it's recommended that you do so for 10 to 15 minutes. This is often impractical because you're forced to exhaust a great deal of your fuel supply. You can opt for chemical treatment, which will kill giardia but will not take care of other chemical pollutants. Another drawback to chemical treatments is the unpleasant taste of the water after it's treated. You can remedy this by adding powdered drink mix to the water. Filters are the preferred method for treating water. Many filters remove giardia and organic and inorganic contaminants, and don't leave an aftertaste. Water filters are far from perfect, as they can easily become clogged or leak if a gasket wears out. It's always a good idea to carry a backup supply of chemical treatment tablets in case your filter decides to quit on you.

Food. If we're talking about survival, you can go days without food, as long as you have water. But we're also talking about comfort. Try to avoid foods that are high in sugar and fat like candy bars and potato chips. These food types are harder to digest and are low in nutritional value. Instead, bring along foods that are easy to pack, nutritious, and high in energy (e.g., bagels, nutrition bars, dehydrated fruit, gorp, and jerky). If you are on an overnight trip, easy-to-fix dinners include rice mixes, dehydrated potatoes, corn, pasta with cheese sauce, and soup mixes. For a tasty breakfast, you can fix hot oatmeal with brown sugar and reconstituted milk powder topped off with banana chips. If you like a hot drink in the morning, bring along herbal tea bags or hot chocolate. If you are a coffee junkie, you can purchase coffee that is packaged like tea bags. You can prepackage all of your meals in heavy-duty resealable plastic bags to keep food from spilling in your pack. These bags can be reused to pack out trash.

Shelter. The type of shelter you choose depends less on the conditions than on your tolerance for discomfort. Shelter comes in many forms—tent, tarp, lean-to, bivy

sack, cabin, cave, etc. If you're camping in the desert, a bivy sack may suffice, but if you're above the tree line and a storm is approaching, a better choice is a three- or four-season tent. Tents are the logical and most popular choice for most backpackers, as they're lightweight and packable—and you can rest assured that you always have shelter from the elements. Before you leave on your trip, anticipate what the weather and terrain will be like and plan for the type of shelter that will work best for your comfort level (see "Equipment" later in this section).

Finding a campsite. If there are established campsites, stick to those. If not, start looking for a campsite early—around 3:30 or 4:00 p.m. Stop at the first decent site you see. Depending on the area, it could be a long time before you find another suitable location. Pitch your camp in an area that's level. Make sure the area is at least 200 feet from fragile areas like lakeshores, meadows, and stream banks. And try to avoid areas thick in underbrush, as they can harbor insects and provide cover for approaching animals.

If you are camping in stormy, rainy weather, look for a rock outcrop or a shelter in the trees to keep the wind from blowing your tent all night. Be sure that you don't camp under trees with dead limbs that might break off on top of you. Also, try to find an area that has an absorbent surface, such as sandy soil or forest duff. This, in addition to camping on a surface with a slight angle, will provide better drainage. By all means, don't dig trenches to provide drainage around your tent—remember you're practicing zero-impact camping.

If you're in bear country, steer clear of creek beds or animal paths. If you see any signs of a bear's presence (i.e., scat, footprints), relocate. You'll need to find a campsite near a tall tree where you can hang your food and other items that may attract bears such as deodorant, toothpaste, or soap. Carry a lightweight nylon rope with which to hang your food. As a rule, you should hang your food at least 20 feet from the ground and 5 feet away from the tree trunk. You can put food and other items in a waterproof stuff sack and tie one end of the rope to the stuff sack. To get the other end of the rope over the tree branch, tie a good-size rock to it and gently toss the rock over the tree branch. Pull the stuff sack up until it reaches the top of the branch and tie it off securely. Don't hang your food near your tent! If possible, hang your food at least 100 feet away from your campsite. Alternatives to hanging your food are bear-proof plastic tubes and metal bear boxes.

Lastly, think of comfort. Lie down on the ground where you intend to sleep and see if it's a good fit. For morning warmth (and a nice view to wake up to), have your tent face east.

First Aid

I know you're tough, but get 10 miles into the woods and develop a blister and you'll wish you had carried that first-aid kit. Face it, it's just plain good sense. Many companies produce lightweight, compact first-aid kits. Just make sure yours contains at least the following:

- Adhesive bandages
- Moleskin or duct tape
- Various sterile gauze and dressings
- White surgical tape
- An ACE bandage
- An antihistamine
- Aspirin
- Ibuprofen or acetaminophen
- Betadine solution
- A first-aid book
- Antacid tablets
- Tweezers
- Scissors
- Antibacterial wipes
- Triple-antibiotic ointment
- Hydrocortisone 1 percent cream
- Plastic gloves
- Sterile cotton tip applicators
- Syrup of ipecac (to induce vomiting)
- Thermometer
- Wire splint

Here are a few tips for dealing with and hopefully preventing certain ailments:

Sunburn. Take along sunscreen or sunblock, protective clothing, and a wide-brimmed hat. If you do get a sunburn, treat the area with aloe vera gel, and protect the area from further sun exposure. At higher elevations the sun's radiation can be particularly damaging to skin. Remember that your eyes are vulnerable to this radiation as well. Sunglasses can be a good way to prevent headaches and permanent eye damage from the sun, especially in places where light-colored rock or patches of snow reflect light up in your face.

Blisters. Be prepared to take care of these hike-spoilers by carrying moleskin (a lightly padded adhesive), gauze and tape, or adhesive bandages. An effective way to apply moleskin is to cut out a circle of moleskin and remove the center—like a doughnut—and place it over the blistered area. Cutting the center out will reduce the pressure applied to the sensitive skin. Other products can help you combat blisters. Some are applied to suspicious hot spots before a blister forms to help decrease friction to that area, while others are applied to the blister after it has popped to help prevent further irritation.

Insect bites and stings. You can treat most insect bites and stings by applying hydrocortisone 1 percent cream topically and taking a pain medication such as ibuprofen or acetaminophen to reduce swelling. If you forgot to pack these items, a cold compress or a paste of mud and ashes can sometimes assuage the itching and discomfort. Remove any stingers by using tweezers or scraping the area with your fingernail or a knife blade. Don't pinch the area, as you'll only spread the venom.

Some hikers are highly sensitive to bites and stings and may have a serious allergic reaction that can be life threatening. Symptoms of a serious allergic reaction can include wheezing, an asthmatic attack, and shock. The treatment for this severe type of reaction is epinephrine. If you know that you are sensitive to bites and stings, carry a prepackaged kit of epinephrine, which can be obtained only by prescription from your doctor.

Ticks. Ticks can carry diseases such as Rocky Mountain spotted fever and Lyme disease. The best defense is, of course, prevention. If you know you're going to be hiking through an area littered with ticks, wear long pants and a long-sleeved shirt. You can apply a permethrin repellent to your clothing and a DEET repellent to exposed skin. At the end of your hike, do a spot check for ticks (and insects in general). If you do find a tick, grab its head firmly—with a pair of tweezers if you have them—and gently pull it away from the skin with a twisting motion. Sometimes the mouthparts linger, embedded in your skin. If this happens, try to remove them with a disinfected needle. Clean the affected area with an antibacterial cleanser and then apply triple antibiotic ointment. Monitor the area for a few days. If irritation persists or a white spot develops, see a doctor for possible infection.

Poison ivy, oak, and sumac. These skin irritants can be found most anywhere in North America and come in the form of a bush or a vine, having leaflets in groups of three, five, seven, or nine. Learn how to spot the plants. The oil they secrete can cause an allergic reaction in the form of blisters, usually about twelve hours after exposure. The itchy rash can last from ten days to several weeks. The best defense against these irritants is to wear clothing that covers the arms, legs and torso. For summer, zip-off cargo pants come in handy. There are also nonprescription lotions you can apply to exposed skin that guard against the effects of poison ivy/oak/sumac and can be washed off with soap and water. If you think you were in contact with the plants, after hiking (or even on the trail during longer hikes) wash with soap and water. Taking a hot shower with soap after you return home from your hike will also help to remove any lingering oil from your skin. Should you contract a rash from any of these plants, use an antihistamine to reduce the itching. If the rash is localized, create a light bleach/water wash to dry up the area. If the rash has spread, either tough it out or see your doctor about getting a dose of cortisone (available both orally and by injection).

Snakebites. Snakebites are rare in North America. Unless startled or provoked, the majority of snakes will not bite. If you are wise to their habitats and keep a careful eye on the trail, you should be just fine. When stepping over logs, first step on the log, making sure you can see what's on the other side before stepping down. Though your chances of being struck are slim, it's wise to know what to do in the event you are.

If a nonpoisonous snake bites you, allow the wound to bleed a small amount and then cleanse the wounded area with a Betadine solution (10 percent povidone iodine). Rinse the wound with clean water (preferably) or fresh urine (it might sound ugly, but it's sterile). Once the area is clean, cover it with triple antibiotic ointment and a clean bandage. Remember, most residual damage from snakebites, poisonous or otherwise, comes from infection, not the snake's venom. Keep the area as clean as possible and get medical attention immediately.

If somebody in your party is bitten by a poisonous snake, follow these steps:

1. Calm the patient.
2. Remove jewelry, watches, and restrictive clothing, and immobilize the affected limb. Do not elevate the injury. Medical opinions vary on whether the area should be lower or level with the heart, but the consensus is that it should not be above it.
3. Make a note of the circumference of the limb at the bite site and at various points above the site as well. This will help you monitor swelling.
4. Evacuate your victim. Ideally he or she should be carried out to minimize movement. If the victim appears to be doing okay, he or she can walk. Stop and rest frequently, and if the swelling appears to be spreading or the patient's symptoms increase, change your plan and find a way to get your patient transported.
5. If you are waiting for rescue, make sure to keep your patient comfortable and hydrated (unless he or she begins vomiting).

Snakebite treatment is rife with old-fashioned remedies: You used to be told to cut and suck the venom out of the bite site or to use a suction cup extractor for the same purpose; applying an electric shock to the area was even in vogue for a while. Do not do any of these things. Do not apply ice, do not give your patient painkillers, and do not apply a tourniquet. All you really want to do is keep your patient calm and get help. If you're alone and have to hike out, don't run—you'll only increase the flow of blood throughout your system. Instead, walk calmly.

Dehydration. Have you ever hiked in hot weather and had a roaring headache and felt fatigued after only a few miles? More than likely you were dehydrated. Symptoms of dehydration include fatigue, headache, and decreased coordination and judgment. When you are hiking, your body's rate of fluid loss depends on the outside temperature, humidity, altitude, and your activity level. On average, a hiker walking in warm weather will lose 4 liters of fluid a day. That fluid loss is easily replaced by normal consumption of liquids and food. However, if a hiker is walking briskly in hot, dry weather and hauling a heavy pack, he or she can lose 1 to 3 liters of water an hour. It's important to always carry plenty of water and to stop often and drink fluids regularly, even if you aren't thirsty.

Heat exhaustion is the result of a loss of large amounts of electrolytes and often occurs if a hiker is dehydrated and has been under heavy exertion. Common symptoms of heat exhaustion include cramping, exhaustion, fatigue, lightheadedness, and nausea. You can treat heat exhaustion by getting out of the sun and drinking an electrolyte solution made up of 1 teaspoon of salt and 1 tablespoon of sugar dissolved in a liter of water. Drink this solution slowly over a period of one hour. Drinking plenty of fluids (preferably an electrolyte solution / sports drink) can prevent heat exhaustion. Avoid hiking during the hottest parts of the day, and wear breathable clothing, a wide-brimmed hat, and sunglasses.

Hypothermia is one of the biggest dangers in the backcountry, especially for day hikers in the summertime. That may sound strange, but imagine starting out on a hike in midsummer when it's sunny and 80 degrees out. You're clad in nylon shorts and a cotton T-shirt. About halfway through your hike, the sky begins to cloud up, and in the next hour a light drizzle begins to fall and the wind starts to pick up. Before you know it, you are soaking wet and shivering—the perfect recipe for hypothermia. More advanced signs include decreased coordination, slurred speech, and blurred vision. When a victim's temperature falls below 92 degrees, the blood pressure and pulse plummet, possibly leading to coma and death.

To avoid hypothermia, always bring a windproof/rainproof shell, a fleece jacket, long underwear made of a breathable synthetic fiber, gloves, and hat when you are hiking in the mountains. Learn to adjust your clothing layers based on the temperature. If you are climbing uphill at a moderate pace you will stay warm, but when you stop for a break you'll become cold quickly, unless you add more layers of clothing.

If a hiker is showing advanced signs of hypothermia, dress him or her in dry clothes and make sure he or she is wearing a hat and gloves. Place the person in a sleeping bag in a tent or shelter that will protect him or her from the wind and other elements. Give the person warm fluids to drink and keep him or her awake.

Frostbite. When the mercury dips below 32 degrees, your extremities begin to chill. If a persistent chill attacks a localized area, say, your hands or your toes, the circulatory system reacts by cutting off blood flow to the affected area—the idea being to protect and preserve the body's overall temperature. And so it's death by attrition for the affected area. Ice crystals start to form from the water in the cells of the neglected tissue. Deprived of heat, nourishment, and now water, the tissue literally starves. This is frostbite.

Prevention is your best defense against this situation. Most prone to frostbite are your face, hands, and feet, so protect these areas well. Wool is the traditional material of choice because it provides ample air space for insulation and draws moisture away from the skin. Synthetic fabrics, however, have made great strides in the cold-weather clothing market. Do your research. A pair of light silk liners under your regular gloves is a good trick for keeping warm. They afford some additional warmth, but more importantly they'll allow you to remove your mitts for tedious work without exposing the skin.

If your feet or hands start to feel cold or numb due to the elements, warm them as quickly as possible. Place cold hands under your armpits or bury them in your crotch. If your feet are cold, change your socks. If there's plenty of room in your boots, add another pair of socks. Do remember, though, that constricting your feet in tight boots can restrict blood flow and actually make your feet colder more quickly. Your socks need to have breathing room if they're going to be effective. Dead air provides insulation. If your face is cold, place your warm hands over your face, or simply wear a head stocking.

Should your skin go numb and start to appear white and waxy, chances are you've got or are developing frostbite. Don't try to thaw the area unless you can maintain the warmth. In other words, don't stop to warm up your frostbitten feet only to head back on the trail. You'll do more damage than good. Tests have shown that hikers who walked on thawed feet did more harm, and endured more pain, than hikers who left the affected areas alone. Do your best to get out of the cold entirely and seek medical attention—which usually consists of performing a rapid rewarming in water for 20 to 30 minutes.

The overall objective in preventing both hypothermia and frostbite is to keep the body's core warm. Protect key areas where heat escapes, like the top of the head, and maintain the proper nutrition level. Foods that are high in calories aid the body in producing heat. Never smoke or drink when you're in situations where the cold is threatening. By affecting blood flow, these activities ultimately cool the body's core temperature.

Hantavirus pulmonary syndrome (HPS). Deer mice spread the virus that causes HPS, and humans contract it from breathing it in, usually when they've disturbed an area with dust and mice feces from nests or surfaces with mice droppings or urine. Exposure to large numbers of rodents and their feces or urine presents the greatest risk. As hikers, we sometimes enter old buildings, and often deer mice live in these places. We may not be around long enough to be exposed, but do be aware of this disease. About half the people who develop HPS die. Symptoms are flulike and appear about two to three weeks after exposure. After initial symptoms, a dry cough and shortness of breath follow. Breathing is difficult. If you even think you might have HPS, see a doctor immediately!

Natural Hazards

Besides tripping over a rock or tree root on the trail, there are some real hazards to be aware of while hiking. Even if where you're hiking doesn't have the plethora of poisonous snakes and plants, insects, and grizzly bears found in other parts of the United States, there are a few weather conditions and predators you may need to take into account.

Lightning. Thunderstorms build over the mountains almost every day during the summer. Lightning is generated by thunderheads and can strike without warning, even several miles away from the nearest overhead cloud. The best rule of thumb is to start leaving exposed peaks, ridges, and canyon rims by about noon. This time can vary a little depending on storm buildup. Keep an eye on cloud formation and don't underestimate how fast a storm can build. The bigger they get, the more likely a thunderstorm will happen.

Lightning takes the path of least resistance, so if you're the high point, it might choose you. Ducking under a rock overhang is dangerous, as you form the shortest path between the rock and ground. If you dash below tree line, avoid standing under the only or the tallest tree. If you are caught above tree line, stay away from anything metal you might be carrying. Move down off the ridge slightly to a low, treeless point and squat until the storm passes. If you have an insulating pad, squat on it. Avoid having both your hands and feet touching the ground at once and never lay flat. If you hear a buzzing sound or feel your hair standing on end, move quickly, as an electrical charge is building up.

Flash floods. Flash floods pose a threat to those hiking near many of the creeks described in this guide. Keep an eye on the weather, and always climb to safety if danger threatens. Flash floods usually subside quickly, so be patient and don't cross a swollen stream.

Bears. Most of the United States (outside of the Pacific Northwest and parts of the Northern Rockies) does not have a grizzly bear population, although some rumors exist about sightings where there should be none. Black bears are plentiful, however. While sightings are rare, there are black bears in Missouri. Here are some tips in case you and a bear scare each other.

Most of all, avoid surprising a bear. Talk or sing where visibility or hearing are limited, such as along a rushing creek or in thick brush. While hiking, watch for bear tracks (five toes), droppings (sizable with leaves, partly digested berries, seeds, and/or animal fur), or rocks and roots along the trail that show signs of being dug up (this could be a bear looking for bugs to eat). Keep a clean camp, hang food or use bear-proof storage containers, and don't sleep in the clothes you wore while cooking. Be especially careful to avoid getting between a mother and her cubs. In late summer and fall, bears are busy eating to fatten up for winter, so be extra careful around berry bushes.

If you do encounter a bear, move away slowly while facing the bear, talk softly, and avoid direct eye contact. Give the bear room to escape. Since bears are very curious, it might stand upright to get a better whiff of you, and it may even charge you to try to intimidate you. Try to stay calm. If a black bear attacks you, fight back with anything you have handy. Unleashed dogs have been known to come running back to their owners with a bear close behind. Keep your dog on a leash or within view at all times.

Mountain lions. It is extremely unlikely that you will see a mountain lion while hiking anywhere in the Midwest. With that being said, there have been a handful of confirmed mountain lion sightings in Missouri in recent years, including one confirmed sighting in St. Louis County in January 2011. Mountain lions appear to be getting more comfortable around humans as long as deer (their favorite prey) are in an area with adequate cover.

Usually elusive and quiet, lions rarely attack people. If you meet a lion, give it a chance to escape. Stay calm and talk firmly to it. Back away slowly while facing the lion. If you run, you'll only encourage the cat to chase you. Make yourself look large by opening a jacket, if you have one, or waving your hiking poles. If the lion behaves aggressively, throw stones, sticks, or whatever you can while remaining tall. If a lion does attack, fight for your life with anything you can grab.

Other considerations. Hunting is a popular sport in the United States, especially during rifle season in October and November. Hiking is still enjoyable in those months in many areas, so just take a few precautions. First, learn when the different hunting seasons start and end in the area in which you'll be hiking. During this time frame, be sure to wear at least a blaze orange hat, and possibly put an orange vest over your pack. Don't be surprised to see hunters in camo outfits carrying bows or rifles around during their season. If you would feel more comfortable without hunters around, hike in national parks and monuments or state and local parks where hunting is not allowed.

Navigation

Whether you are going on a short hike in a familiar area or planning a weeklong backpack trip, you should always be equipped with the proper navigational equipment—at the very least a detailed map and a sturdy compass.

Maps. There are many different types of maps available to help you find your way on the trail. Easiest to find are Forest Service maps and BLM (Bureau of Land Management) maps. These maps tend to cover large areas, so be sure they are detailed enough for your particular trip. You can also obtain national park maps as well as high-quality maps from private companies and trail groups. These maps can be obtained either from outdoor stores or ranger stations.

US Geological Survey topographic maps are particularly popular with hikers—especially serious backcountry hikers. These maps contain the standard map symbols such as roads, lakes, and rivers, as well as contour lines that show the details of the trail terrain like ridges, valleys, passes, and mountain peaks. The 7.5-minute series (1 inch on the map equals approximately 0.4 mile on the ground) provides the closest inspection available. Visit https://store.usgs.gov/maps.

The art of map reading is a skill that you can develop by first practicing in an area you are familiar with. To begin, orient the map so it is lined up in the correct direction (i.e., north on the map is lined up with true north). Next, familiarize yourself with the map symbols and try to match them up with terrain features around you such as a high ridge, mountain peak, river, or lake. If you are practicing with a USGS map, notice the contour lines. On gentler terrain these contour lines are spaced farther apart, and on steeper terrain they are closer together. Pick a short loop trail, and stop frequently to check your position on the map. As you practice map reading, you'll learn how to anticipate a steep section on the trail or a good place to take a rest break, and so on.

Compasses. First off, the sun is not a substitute for a compass. So, what kind of compass should you have? Here are some characteristics you should look for: a rectangular base with detailed scales, a liquid-filled housing, a protective housing, a sighting line on the mirror, luminous alignment and back-bearing arrows, a luminous north-seeking arrow, and a well-defined bezel ring.

You can learn compass basics by reading the detailed instructions included with your compass. If you want to fine-tune your compass skills, sign up for an orienteering class or purchase a book on compass reading. Once you've learned the basic skills of using a compass, remember to practice these skills before you head into the backcountry.

GPS (Global Positioning System) devices. If you are a klutz at using a compass, you may be interested in checking out the technical wizardry of a GPS device. GPS was developed by the Pentagon and works off twenty-four NAVSTAR satellites, which were designed to guide missiles to their targets. A GPS device is a handheld unit that calculates your latitude and longitude with the easy press of a button. The Department of Defense used to scramble the satellite signals a bit to prevent civilians (and spies!) from getting extremely accurate readings, but that practice was discontinued in May 2000, and GPS units now provide nearly pinpoint accuracy (within 25 feet).

There are many different types of GPS units available. In general, all GPS units have a display screen and keypad where you input information. In addition to acting as a compass, the unit allows you to plot your route, easily retrace your path, track your traveling speed, find the mileage between waypoints, and calculate the total mileage of your route.

Before you purchase a GPS unit, keep in mind that these devices don't pick up signals indoors, in heavily wooded areas, on mountain peaks, or in deep valleys. Also, batteries can wear out or other technical problems can develop. A GPS unit should be used in conjunction with a map and compass, not in place of those items.

Pedometers. A pedometer is a small, clip-on unit with a digital display that calculates your hiking distance in miles or kilometers based on your walking stride. Some units also calculate the calories you burn and your total hiking time. Pedometers are available at most large outdoor stores.

Trip Planning

Planning your hiking adventure begins with letting friends or relatives know your trip itinerary so they can call for help if you don't return at your scheduled time. Your next task is to make sure you are outfitted to experience the risks and rewards of the trail. This section highlights gear and clothing you may want to take with you to get the most out of your hike.

Day Hikes

- [ ] Camera
- [ ] Compass / GPS unit
- [ ] Daypack
- [ ] First–aid kit
- [ ] Fleece jacket
- [ ] Food
- [ ] Guidebook
- [ ] Hat
- [ ] Headlamp/flashlight with extra batteries and bulbs
- [ ] Insect repellent
- [ ] Knife / multipurpose tool
- [ ] Map
- [ ] Matches in waterproof container and fire starter
- [ ] Pedometer
- [ ] Rain gear
- [ ] Space blanket
- [ ] Sunglasses
- [ ] Sunscreen
- [ ] Swimsuit and/or fishing gear (if hiking to a lake)
- [ ] Watch
- [ ] Water
- [ ] Water bottles / water hydration system

Overnight Trip

- [ ] Backpack and waterproof rain cover
- [ ] Backpacker's trowel
- [ ] Bandanna
- [ ] Bear canister or rope to hang food
- [ ] Biodegradable soap
- [ ] Clothing—extra wool socks, shirt, and shorts
- [ ] Collapsible water container (2- to 3-gallon capacity)
- [ ] Cook set / utensils
- [ ] Ditty bags to store gear

- [ ] Extra plastic resealable bags
- [ ] Gaiters
- [ ] Garbage bag
- [ ] Ground cloth
- [ ] Journal/pen
- [ ] Long underwear
- [ ] Nylon rope to hang food
- [ ] Permit (if required)
- [ ] Pot scrubber
- [ ] Rain jacket and pants
- [ ] Sandals to wear around camp and to ford streams
- [ ] Sleeping bag
- [ ] Sleeping pad
- [ ] Small bath towel
- [ ] Stove and fuel
- [ ] Tent
- [ ] Toiletry items
- [ ] Water filter
- [ ] Waterproof stuff sack
- [ ] Whistle

Equipment

With the outdoor market currently flooded with products, many of which are pure gimmickry, it seems impossible to both differentiate and choose. Do I really need a tropical-fish-lined collapsible shower? (No, you don't.) The only defense against the maddening quantity of items thrust in your face is to think practically—and to do so before you go shopping. The worst buys are impulsive buys. Since most name brands will differ only slightly in quality, it's best to know what you're looking for in terms of function. Buy only what you need. You will, don't forget, be carrying what you've bought on your back. Here are some things to keep in mind before you go shopping.

Clothes. Clothing is your armor against Mother Nature's little surprises. Hikers should be prepared for any possibility, especially when hiking in mountainous areas. Adequate rain protection and extra layers of clothing are a good idea. In summer a wide-brimmed hat can help keep the sun at bay. In the winter months the first layer you'll want to wear is a "wicking" layer of long underwear that keeps perspiration away from your skin. Wear long underwear made from synthetic fibers that wick moisture away from the skin and draw it toward the next layer of clothing, where it then evaporates. Avoid wearing long underwear made of cotton, as it is slow to dry and keeps moisture next to your skin.

The second layer you'll wear is the "insulating" layer. Aside from keeping you warm, this layer needs to "breathe" so you stay dry while hiking. A fabric that provides insulation and dries quickly is fleece. It's interesting to note that this one-of-a-kind fabric is made out of recycled plastic. Purchasing a zip-up jacket made of this material is highly recommended.

The last line of layering defense is the "shell" layer. You'll need some type of waterproof, windproof, breathable jacket that will fit over all of your other layers. It should have a large hood that fits over a hat. You'll also need a good pair of rain pants made from a similar waterproof, breathable fabric. Some Gore-Tex jackets cost as much as $1,000, but you should know that there are more affordable fabrics out there that work just as well.

Now that you've learned the basics of layering, you can't forget to protect your hands and face. In cold, windy, or rainy weather you'll need a hat made of wool or fleece and insulated, waterproof gloves that will keep your hands warm and toasty. As mentioned earlier, buying an additional pair of light silk liners to wear under your regular gloves is a good idea.

Footwear. If you have any extra money to spend on your trip, put that money into boots or trail shoes. Poor shoes will bring a hike to a halt faster than anything else. To avoid this annoyance, buy shoes that provide support and are lightweight and flexible. A lightweight hiking boot is better than a heavy, leather mountaineering boot for most day hikes and backpacking. Trail running shoes provide a little extra cushion and are made in a high-top style that many people wear for hiking. These running shoes are lighter, more flexible, and more breathable than hiking boots. If you know you'll be hiking in wet weather often, purchase boots or shoes with a Gore-Tex liner, which will help keep your feet dry.

When buying your boots, be sure to wear the same type of socks you'll be wearing on the trail. If the boots you're buying are for cold-weather hiking, try the boots on while wearing two pairs of socks. Speaking of socks, a good cold-weather sock combination is to wear a thinner sock made of wool or polypropylene covered by a heavier outer sock made of wool or a synthetic/wool mix. The inner sock protects the foot from the rubbing effects of the outer sock and prevents blisters. Many outdoor stores have some type of ramp to simulate hiking uphill and downhill. Be sure to take advantage of this test, as toe-jamming boot fronts can be very painful and debilitating on the downhill trek.

Once you've purchased your footwear, be sure to break them in before you hit the trail. New footwear is often stiff and needs to be stretched and molded to your foot.

Hiking poles. Hiking poles help with balance, and more importantly take pressure off your knees. The ones with shock absorbers are easier on your elbows and knees. Some poles even come with a camera attachment to be used as a monopod. And heaven forbid you meet a mountain lion, bear, or unfriendly dog, the poles can make you look a lot bigger.

Backpacks. No matter what type of hiking you do, you'll need a pack of some sort to carry the basic trail essentials. There are a variety of backpacks on the market, but let's first discuss what you intend to use it for: day hikes or overnight trips?

If you plan on doing a day hike, a daypack should have some of the following characteristics: a padded hip belt that's at least 2 inches in diameter (avoid packs with only a small nylon piece of webbing for a hip belt); a chest strap (the chest strap helps stabilize the pack against your body); external pockets to carry water and other items that you want easy access to; an internal pocket to hold keys, a knife, a wallet, and other miscellaneous items; an external lashing system to hold a jacket; and, if you so desire, a hydration pocket for carrying a hydration system (which consists of a water bladder with an attachable drinking hose).

For short hikes, some hikers like to use a small, lightweight daypacks to store just a camera, food, a compass, a map, and other trail essentials. Most of these lightweight daypacks have pockets for two water bottles and areas to store cellphones, snacks, and other items you will want to access easily.

If you intend to do an extended, overnight trip, there are multiple considerations. First off, you need to decide what kind of framed pack you want. There are two backpack types for backpacking: the internal frame and the external frame. An internal frame pack rests closer to your body, making it more stable and easier to balance when hiking over rough terrain. An external frame pack is just that, an aluminum frame attached to the exterior of the pack. Some hikers consider an external frame pack to be better for long backpack trips because it distributes the pack weight better and allows you to carry heavier loads. It's often easier to pack, and your gear is more accessible. It also offers better back ventilation in hot weather.

The most critical measurement for fitting a pack is torso length. The pack needs to rest evenly on your hips without sagging. A good pack will come in two or three sizes and have straps and hip belts that are adjustable according to your body size and characteristics.

When you purchase a backpack, go to an outdoor store with salespeople who are knowledgeable in how to properly fit a pack. Once the pack is fitted for you, load it with the amount of weight you plan on taking on the trail. The weight of the pack should be distributed evenly, and you should be able to swing your arms and walk briskly without feeling out of balance. Another good technique for evaluating a pack is to walk up and down stairs and make quick turns to the right and to the left to be sure the pack doesn't feel out of balance. Other features that are nice to have on a backpack include a removable daypack or fanny pack, external pockets for extra water, and extra lash points to attach a jacket or other items.

Sleeping bags and pads. Sleeping bags are rated by temperature. You can purchase a bag made with synthetic insulation, or you can buy a goose down bag. Goose down bags are more expensive, but they have a higher insulating capacity by weight and will keep their loft longer. You'll want to purchase a bag with a temperature rating that fits the time of year and conditions you are most likely to camp in. One caveat: The techno-standard for temperature ratings is far from perfect. Ratings vary from manufacturer to manufacturer, so to protect yourself you should purchase a bag rated 10 to 15 degrees below the temperature you expect to be camping in. Synthetic

bags are more resistant to water than down bags, but many down bags are now made with a Gore-Tex shell that helps to repel water. Down bags are also more compressible than synthetic bags and take up less room in your pack, which is an important consideration if you are planning a multiday backpack trip. Features to look for in a sleeping bag include a mummy-style bag, a hood you can cinch down around your head in cold weather, and draft tubes along the zippers that help keep heat in and drafts out.

You'll also want a sleeping pad to provide insulation and padding from the cold ground. There are different types of sleeping pads available, from the more expensive self-inflating air mattresses to the less expensive closed-cell foam pads. Self-inflating air mattresses are usually heavier than closed-cell foam mattresses and are prone to punctures.

Tents. The tent is your home away from home while on the trail. It provides protection from wind, rain, snow, and insects. A three-season tent is a good choice for backpacking. These lightweight and versatile tents provide protection in all types of weather, except heavy snowstorms or high winds, and range in weight from 4 to 8 pounds. Look for a tent that's easy to set up and will easily fit two people with gear. Dome-type tents usually offer more headroom and places to store gear. Other handy tent features include a vestibule where you can store wet boots and backpacks. Some nice-to-have items in a tent include interior pockets to store small items and lashing points to hang a clothesline. Most three-season tents also come with stakes so you can secure the tent in high winds. Before you purchase a tent, set it up and take it down a few times to be sure it is easy to handle. Also, sit inside the tent and make sure it has enough room for you and your gear.

Cellphones. Many hikers are carrying their cellphones into the backcountry these days in case of emergency. That's fine and good, but please know that cellphone coverage is often poor to nonexistent in valleys, canyons, and thick forest. More importantly, people have started to call for help because they're tired or lost. Let's go back to being prepared. You are responsible for yourself in the backcountry. Use your brain to avoid problems, and if you do encounter one, first use your brain to try to correct the situation. Only use your cellphone, if it works, in true emergencies. If it doesn't work down low in a valley, try hiking to a high point where you might get reception.

Hiking with Children

Hiking with children isn't a matter of how many miles you can cover or how much elevation gain you make in a day; it's about seeing and experiencing nature through their eyes.

Kids like to explore and have fun. They like to stop and point out bugs and plants, look under rocks, jump in puddles, and throw sticks. If you're taking a toddler or young child on a hike, start with a trail that you're familiar with. Trails that have interesting things for kids, like piles of leaves to play in or a small stream to wade through during the summer, will make the hike much more enjoyable for them and will keep them from getting bored.

You can keep your child's attention if you have a strategy before starting on the trail. Using games is not only an effective way to keep a child's attention, it's also a great way to teach him or her about nature. Quiz children on the names of plants and animals. Pick up a family-friendly outdoor hobby like geocaching (www.geocaching .com) or Letterboxing (www.atlasquest.com), both of which combine the outdoors, clue-solving, and treasure hunting. If your children are old enough, let them carry their own daypack filled with snacks and water. So that you are sure to go at their pace and not yours, let them lead the way. Playing follow the leader works particularly well when you have a group of children. Have each child take a turn at being the leader.

With children, a lot of clothing is key. The only thing predictable about weather is that it will change. Especially in mountainous areas, weather can change dramatically in a very short time. Always bring extra clothing for children, regardless of the season. In the winter have your children wear wool socks and warm layers such as long underwear, a fleece jacket and hat, wool mittens, and good rain gear. It's not a bad idea to have these along in late fall and early spring as well. Good footwear is also important. A sturdy pair of high-top tennis shoes or lightweight hiking boots are the best bet for little ones. If you're hiking in the summer near a lake or stream, bring along a pair of old sneakers that your child can put on when he or she wants to go exploring in the water. Remember when you're near any type of water, watch your child at all times. Also, keep a close eye on teething toddlers who may decide a rock or leaf of poison oak is an interesting item to put in their mouth.

From spring through fall, you'll want your kids to wear a wide-brimmed hat to keep their face, head, and ears protected from the hot sun. Also, make sure your children wear sunscreen at all times. Choose a brand without PABA—children have sensitive skin and may have an allergic reaction to sunscreen that contains PABA. If you are hiking with a child younger than six months, don't use sunscreen or insect repellent. Instead, be sure that their head, face, neck, and ears are protected from the sun with a wide-brimmed hat, and that all other skin exposed to the sun is protected with the appropriate clothing.

Remember that food is fun. Kids like snacks, so it's important to bring a lot of munchies for the trail. Stopping often for snack breaks is a fun way to keep the trail interesting. Raisins, apples, granola bars, crackers and cheese, cereal, and trail mix all make great snacks. Also, a few of their favorite candy treats can go a long way toward heading off a fit of fussing. If your children are old enough to carry their own backpack, let them fill it with some lightweight "comfort" items such as a doll, a small stuffed animal, or a little toy (you'll have to draw the line at bringing the 10-pound Tonka truck). If your kids don't like drinking water, you can bring some powdered drink mix or a juice box.

Avoid poorly designed child-carrying packs—you don't want to break your back carrying your child. Most child-carrying backpacks designed to hold a 40-pound child will contain a large carrying pocket to hold diapers and other items. Some have an optional rain/sun hood.

Hiking with Your Dog

Bringing your furry friend with you is always more fun than leaving him behind. Our canine pals make great trail buddies because they never complain and always make good company. Hiking with your dog can be a rewarding experience, especially if you plan ahead. Keep in mind that national parks and many wilderness areas do not allow dogs on trails. Your best bet is to hike in national forests, BLM lands, and state parks. Always call ahead to see what the restrictions are.

Getting your dog in shape. Before you plan outdoor adventures with your dog, make sure he's in shape for the trail. Getting your dog into shape takes the same discipline as getting yourself into shape, but luckily your dog can get in shape with you. Take your dog with you on your daily runs or walks. If there is a park near your house, hit a tennis ball or play Frisbee with your dog.

Swimming is also an excellent way to get your dog into shape. If there is a lake or river near where you live and your dog likes the water, have him retrieve a tennis ball or stick. Gradually build your dog's stamina up over a two- to three-month period. A good rule of thumb is to assume that your dog will travel twice as far as you will on the trail. If you plan on doing a 5-mile hike, be sure your dog is in shape for a 10-mile hike.

Training your dog for the trail. Before you go on your first hiking adventure with your dog, be sure he has a firm grasp on the basics of canine etiquette and behavior. Make sure he can sit, lie down, stay, and come. One of the most important commands you can teach your canine pal is to "come" under any situation. It's easy for your friend's nose to lead him astray or possibly get lost. Another helpful command is the "get behind" command. When you're on a hiking trail that's narrow, you can have your dog follow behind you when other trail users approach. Nothing is more bothersome than an enthusiastic dog that runs back and forth on the trail and disrupts the peace of the trail for others—or, worse, jumps up on other hikers and gets them muddy. When you see other trail users approaching you on the trail, give them the right-of-way by quietly stepping off the trail and making your dog lie down and stay until they pass.

Equipment. The most critical pieces of equipment you can invest in for your dog are proper identification and a sturdy leash. Flexi-leads work well for hiking because they give your dog more freedom to explore but still leave you in control. Make sure your dog has identification that includes your name and address and a number for your veterinarian. Other forms of identification for your dog include a tattoo or a microchip. You should consult your veterinarian for more information on these last two options.

The next piece of equipment you'll want to consider is a pack for your dog. By no means should you hold all of your dog's essentials in your pack—let him carry his own gear! Dogs that are in good shape can carry 30 to 40 percent of their own weight. Most packs are fitted by a dog's weight and girth measurement. Companies that make dog packs generally include guidelines to help you pick out the size that's right for your dog. Some characteristics to look for when purchasing a pack for your dog include a harness that contains two padded girth straps, a padded chest strap, leash attachments, removable saddle bags, internal water bladders, and external gear cords.

You can introduce your dog to the pack by first placing the empty pack on his back and letting him wear it around the yard. Keep an eye on him during this first introduction. He may decide to chew through the straps if you aren't watching him closely. Once he learns to treat the pack as an object of fun and not a foreign enemy, fill the pack evenly on both sides with a few ounces of dog food in resealable plastic bags. Have your dog wear his pack on your daily walks for a period of two to three weeks. Each week add a little more weight to the pack until your dog will accept carrying the maximum amount of weight he can carry.

You can also purchase collapsible water and dog food bowls for your dog. These bowls are lightweight and can easily be stashed into your pack or your dog's. If you are hiking on rocky terrain or in the snow, you can purchase footwear for your dog that will protect his feet from cuts and bruises.

Always carry plastic bags to remove feces from the trail. It is a courtesy to other trail users and helps protect local wildlife.

The following is a list of items to bring when you take your dog hiking: collapsible bowls, a comb, a collar and a leash, dog food, plastic bags for feces, a dog pack, flea/tick powder, paw protection, water, and a first-aid kit that contains eye ointment, tweezers, scissors, stretchy foot wrap, gauze, antibacterial wash, sterile cotton tip applicators, antibiotic ointment, and cotton wrap.

First aid for your dog. Your dog is just as prone—if not more prone—to getting in trouble on the trail as you are, so be prepared. Here's a rundown of the more likely misfortunes that might befall your little friend:

Bees and wasps. If a bee or wasp stings your dog, remove the stinger with a pair of tweezers and place a mudpack or a cloth dipped in cold water over the affected area.

Porcupines. One good reason to keep your dog on a leash is to prevent him from getting a nose full of porcupine quills. You may be able to remove the quills with pliers, but a veterinarian is the best person to do this nasty job because most dogs need to be sedated.

Heat stroke. Avoid hiking with your dog in really hot weather. Dogs with heat stroke will pant excessively, lie down and refuse to get up, and become lethargic and disoriented. If your dog shows any of these signs on the trail, have him lie down in the shade. If you are near a stream, pour cool water over your dog's entire body to help bring his body temperature back to normal.

Heartworm. Dogs get heartworms from mosquitoes that carry the disease in the prime mosquito months of July and August. Giving your dog a monthly pill prescribed by your veterinarian easily prevents this condition.

Plant pitfalls. If you have a long-haired dog, consider trimming the hair between his toes and giving him a summer haircut to help prevent plants from becoming tangled in your dog's fur. After every hike look over your dog for thorns, thistles, burrs, and other seeds—especially between his toes and his ears. If you find any burrs or thistles on your dog, remove them as soon as possible before they become an unmanageable mat. Thorns can pierce a dog's foot and cause a great deal of pain. If you see that your dog is lame, stop and check his feet for thorns.

Another plant hazard is poison ivy. Dogs are not immune to poison ivy, and they can pick up the sticky, oily substance from the plant and transfer it to you.

Protect those paws. Be sure to keep your dog's nails trimmed so he avoids getting soft tissue or joint injuries. If your dog slows and refuses to go on, check to see that his paws aren't torn or worn. You can protect your dog's paws from trail hazards such as sharp gravel and thorns by purchasing dog boots. Ruffwear makes an excellent pair that is both sturdy and stays on the dog's feet.

Sunburn. If your dog has light skin, he is an easy target for sunburn on his nose and other exposed skin areas. You can apply a nontoxic sunscreen to exposed skin areas that will help protect him from overexposure to the sun.

Ticks and fleas. Ticks can easily give your dog Lyme disease, as well as other diseases. Before you hit the trail, treat your dog with a flea and tick spray or powder. You can also use a once-a-month pour-on treatment that repels fleas and ticks. Oral flea and tick prevention is also available.

Creeping myrtle

Mosquitoes and deerflies. These little flying machines can do a job on your dog's snout and ears. Best bet is to spray your dog with fly repellent for horses to discourage both pests.

Giardia. Dogs can get giardiasis, which results in diarrhea. It is usually not debilitating, but it's definitely messy.

Mushrooms. Make sure your dog doesn't sample mushrooms along the trail. They could be poisonous to him, but he doesn't know that.

Hike Index

About the Authors

JD Tanner grew up playing and exploring in the hills of southern Illinois. He earned a degree in outdoor recreation from Southeast Missouri State University and an advanced degree in outdoor recreation from Southern Illinois University in Carbondale. He has traveled extensively throughout the United States and is the director at Southern Illinois University's Touch of Nature Environmental Center.

Emily Ressler–Tanner grew up splitting time between southeastern Missouri and southeastern Idaho. She spent her early years fishing, hiking, and camping with her family. In college she enjoyed trying out many new outdoor activities and eventually graduated from Southern Illinois University with an advanced degree in recreation resource administration.

Together Emily and JD have climbed, hiked, paddled, and camped their way across the United States. They co-instructed college-level outdoor recreation courses for several years before joining the staff at the Leave No Trace Center for Outdoor Ethics as traveling trainers. They currently reside in southern Illinois.

Emily and JD have written or revised these FalconGuides:

Best Easy Day Hikes Grand Staircase—Escalante (Revised)

Best Easy Day Hikes Missouri Ozarks

Best Easy Day Hikes Springfield, Missouri

Best Easy Day Hikes St. Louis

Best Easy Day Hikes Four Corners

Best Hikes Near Albuquerque

Best Hikes Near St. Louis

Best Bike Rides Albuquerque and Santa Fe

Hiking the Four Corners

Hiking the Ozarks

Hiking Grand Staircase—Escalante (Revised)